The HIGHLAND CLANS

The HIGHLAND CLANS

ALISTAIR MOFFAT

with 86 illustrations, 35 in color

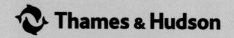

Thames & Hudson

For Norman Gillies

PAGE 1 Woodcut depicting the Scottish thistle, official emblem of Scotland.

PAGE 2 Pipe-Major MacDonald, 72nd Regiment of Foot.

PAGE 4 Highland Games in London, 1937.

First published in 2010 in hardcover in the United States of America by Thames & Hudson Inc., 500 Fifth Avenue, New York, New York 10110

thamesandhudsonusa.com

First paperback edition 2013

Library of Congress Catalog Card Number 2009935639

ISBN 978-0-500-29084-2

Printed and bound in China by Hung Hing Offset Printing Company Ltd

CONTENTS

PREFACE: **THE CHILDREN OF THE MIST** 6

1 • **THE NAMES OF HIS BLOOD** 8

2 • **AT FIRST LIGHT THE STANDARDS GLEAMED** 15

3 • **OUT OF THE MOUTH OF THE MORNING** 26

4 • **THE AGE OF THE FORAYS** 41

5 • **THE CLANS DAUNTED** 51

6 • **NO FURTHER THAN HERE** 64

7 • **MOMENTS WHEN NOTHING SEEMED IMPOSSIBLE** 75

8 • **LOCHABER NO MORE** 106

9 • **THE BLOOD IS STRONG** 132

10 • **CAMUSDARROCH** 142

11 • **THE CLANS** 147

SOURCES OF ILLUSTRATIONS 174

FURTHER READING 175

INDEX 175

40 kilometres

20 miles

Shapinsay

Rousay
Stronsay

Orkney Islands

Hoy

MacKay

Sinclair

Oliphant

MacLeod

SUTHERLAND

Gunn

Mackenzie

Morrison

Mathieson

MacAulay Stornoway

MacAskill

MACLEOD

Lewis

Western Isles

MacDonell

Harris

MacLeod

ROSS

Munro

Rose   *Brodie*   *Innes*   *Cumming*

Culloden 1746

Keith

North Uist

MACDONALD

Loch
Maree

Urquhart

MACKENZIE

Bembecula

MacLeod

MacCrimmon

MacKinnon

Skye

Fraser

Chisholm

INVERNESS

Mackintosh   *Grant*

MacBain

GORDON

Forbes

ABERDEEN

MacDonald

South Uist

MacLennan

Grant

Clan Chattan

Menzies

Burnett   *Burnett*

MacNeil

Barra

MacDonald of
Clan Ranald

Rum

Eigg

MacDonell of
Glengarry

MacDonell
of Keppoch

CAMERON

MacPherson

Stewart

Farquharson

Keith

Lindsay

Glenfinnan

MacDonald

Robertson

Killiecrankie
1689

Graham

Coll

Tiree

MacLean   MacKinnon

Staffa   *Mull*

MacLean

Iona

MacInnes

Stewart

CAMPBELL

MacArthur

MacDougall

MacNab

MacLaren

MacGregor

Menzies

Murray

Ogilvie

DUNDEE

PERTH

Hay   *MacDuff*

Drummond   *Rollo*

Erskine   *Lindsay*

Sheriffmuir 1715

MacFarlane

STIRLING

Campbell

MacLachlan

Buchanan

MacFie

Colonsay

MacLean

Jura

MacMillan

Campbell

Islay   Beaton

MacDonald

Gigha

MacEwan
Lamont

Colquhoun

Bannockburn
1314

Bruce

Prestonpans 1745

Seton

EDINBURGH

Stewart

GLASGOW

Livingstone

Hay

Montgomerie

Cunningham

Hay

Arran

MacDonell

Wallace

NORTHERN IRELAND

Ferguson

ENGLAND

THE CHILDREN OF THE MIST

WITHOUT THEIR NAMES THE HIGHLAND CLANS WERE NOTHING, NO BETTER THAN LOWLANDERS OR THE ENGLISH. Much more than mere labels, names were also addresses, pinning people to the rugged map of northern Scotland, to their own straths and glens. This was the kindred ground, the places where communities with the same surname had farmed, fished and hunted for many generations. Clan lands sometimes moved or were taken by force by others, but most of the famous names remained in their ancient places.

Clan is from *clann*, the Gaelic word for children. Clansmen and women saw themselves as descended from common name-fathers, often distant ancestors who in some meaningful sense were the first of that name. And so Clan Donald were originally the children of Donald. When they called themselves MacDonalds they allowed no doubt that lineage was the exclusive concern of men for the prefix *mac* means son of. Alternative words for clan underscore the paternalistic history of the great names. *Siol* means seed or sperm and *sliochd* is offspring. *Siol Diarmaid* was an old name for Clan Campbell and the MacLeods of Lewis were also known as *Siol Torcuil*.

The origins of a few of the clans are very old, reaching far back into the uncertainties of the Dark Ages, but many name-fathers had real historical personalities and those men usually emerged some time between 1150 and 1350. For half a millennium and more the clans were very powerful and their chiefs ruled the Highlands of Scotland with little hindrance. But after the last of the Jacobite rebellions in 1745 and the great emigrations of the 18th and 19th centuries, when clansmen and women disappeared into the crowded streets of big cities or were scattered to the corners of the Earth, their power shrivelled and the names became little more than memories.

In the remote and empty glens herds of wild deer roam and their habit of appearing as if from nowhere is described in a Gaelic phrase. Descending from the mountains and the high passes, the deer are called *Clann a' Cheo*, the Children of the Mist. Travellers in the north of Scotland might think of the clans in the same way, their history only occasionally glimpsed in the distance, fleeting, disappearing into the dense forest and the heather-clad uplands. But it is there, and it is a wonderful, magical story.

OPPOSITE *The locations of clan lands and battle sites.*

1

THE NAMES OF HIS BLOOD

HERE WOULD BE A BATTLE, AND SOON. It was to be the last battle, although no one could know it at the time, the last pitched battle to be fought on British soil. Murdoch MacLeod had watched the clan regiments converge on Inverness for two months. Now the government army was not far behind, approaching fast on the east road, it was said, and its supporting fleet had been sighted in the Moray Firth. With no further retreat possible, Prince Charles would have to turn his undefeated Highland army and make a stand. At Prestonpans and Falkirk their fearless and furious charges had scattered the redcoats and slaughtered them in their hundreds as they ran for their lives. There would be a battle, another certain victory for the clans and their rightful king. And when it came Murdoch MacLeod was determined to fight, determined on glory. He was 15 years old.

ABOVE *Prince Charles Edward Stuart, more commonly known as Bonnie Prince Charlie, the charismatic leader of the rebellion of 1745–46.*

On 15 April 1746 the clans mustered on Drummossie Moor, near Culloden House, about six miles east of Inverness. The town was aflame with the news that battle would be joined the following day. Murdoch made his plans. Instead of going to the grammar school he hurried away east out of the town. Somehow he acquired a broadsword, a shield and a dirk, perhaps taking them from a bivouac of sleeping

ABOVE *A near-contemporary print of the Battle of Culloden, which took place in 1746, with Culloden House in the background. Depicted as a rout – and a surprising attack on Jacobite women – the composition allows no doubt about the outcome.*

clansmen. Murdoch may have been a schoolboy playing truant, but in his secret heart he was a warrior, a clansman. When the time came he would remember who he was and fight for the Prince, and for his own people. He would be a MacLeod.

It began to rain, a slanting cold rain billowing out of the west over the dark heads of the mountains. When Murdoch at last reached Drummossie Moor nothing could have prepared the boy for the enormity of what he saw. Two armies faced each other. Regiments of redcoats stood in line, many of their officers on horseback behind them, and batteries of black cannon emplaced at regular intervals. Drums rattled and orders were called out over the morning moor. 'Stand fast and look to your fronts' roared the sergeants. The Duke of Cumberland rode up and down with his aides, stopping occasionally to put a spyglass to his eye, to try to make out through the rain what the rabble of savages facing his men were doing.

When Murdoch walked out onto the battlefield he saw the clans standing in battle order. Drawn up in lines, the men were neither drilled nor in uniform, but clustered in family groups. Fathers were with their sons, brothers stood together, cousins and uncles stayed close, many of the officers standing forward of the front rank were related to the men at their back. The oldest and most experienced were always set to the front, for the clansmen believed that courage flowed down the generations. Prince Charles led an army of families, of men joined by blood and obligation. And Murdoch looked up and down the battle front for the MacLeods. He wanted to stand with the names of his blood.

Perhaps they could be found by their music. At the head of each clan the war pipes skirled out the battle rants, each of them different, many remembering the victories of the past. On the right of the line, under the command of Lord George Murray, the Atholl Brigade had been allotted the place of honour. Robertsons, Murrays, Menzies and a scattering of MacGregors from Perthshire and the Southern Highlands stared across the heather at the hated redcoats, only 500 yards away. To the left of Atholl were Locheil's men, Camerons from Lochaber and the seaward lands of the Great Glen, among the first to rally to the Prince's standard at Glenfinnan a year before. Seven hundred waited for their chief to roar 'Claidheamh Mòr!', the order to charge.

BELOW *Described as 'An Incident in the Battle of Culloden', David Morier's painting depicts a rabble of savages on the left being repelled by the stern bristle of disciplined government steel on the right.*

Beside them, the Stewarts of Appin, from the fertile low country to the east of the Firth of Lorne, were also growing restive. There was a regiment of Campbells in the government army, their treacherous and protestant southern neighbours who had plundered Stewart glens and reived Stewart cattle. Culloden was a battle for a kingdom, no doubt, but it was also a battle between clans. Charles Stewart of Ardshiel was tutor to the chief, who was still a child, and he had the honour of leading the charge of the Appin men. A great swordsman, and tall, he would be the first of his name to reach the enemy. With the Stewarts stood their client clans: MacColls, Carmichaels, Livingstones and MacLays. Pinned to their bonnets each man wore a sprig of green oak leaves, their clan badge. Lord George and the Atholl Brigade had cut sprigs of broom and the Lochaber men also wore oak. All wore plaids, soaked through by now, but none could be recognized by a distinctive tartan. Many men wore more than one sett. And all had the white cockade, a rosette of white ribbon for the Jacobite cause, in prominent show.

Lord John Drummond commanded the centre. Behind him was the Fraser regiment, 300 men expecting to be reinforced by Lord Lovat's company. He was hurrying to Inverness on the morning of the battle, but his men would never reach the

ABOVE *Lord George Murray (1694–1760) preferred a kilt to tartan riding trews so that he could march with his men.*

moor. Like the Menzies and the Grants, the Frasers were a Norman-French clan, descended from 12th-century plantations of immigrants in the north, and *Friseil*, the Gaelic version of the name, betrays the derivation from *La Frezelière*, a lordship in Anjou.

Few of the Norse clans of the Western Isles came out for the Prince in 1745. Murdoch would find some MacLeods at Culloden but few MacSweens, MacIvors or MacAulays, the ancient sons of Swein, Ivar and Olaf. But the Wildcats were there: the old Pictish confederacy of Clan Chattan was drawn up next to the Frasers. They were Mackintoshes, MacBains, MacGillivrays and Farquharsons from Balmoral and some were fighting on that terrible day on their clan lands. Beyond the ranks of the Wildcats were small regiments of MacLeans from Mull and Sunart, and Chisholms from the high mountain country west of Loch Ness. They were led by a priest, Donald Chisholm, for the chief, MacIain, was too old to fight. One of his sons, Ruaridh Og, led a clan company while two of his older brothers had joined the Royal Scots and enlisted in the government army. Culloden was also a battle between families.

On the left wing, and insulted to be there, stood the MacDonald regiments: Glengarry, Keppoch and Clan Ranald. Their chiefs had once been Lords of the Isles, the great Atlantic principality of the clans, and after helping Robert the Bruce to victory at Bannockburn in 1314, they had held the place of honour in Scottish battle lines for four centuries. But not on that day. And because of the ground the men of Clan Donald stood some way further back, 700 yards from the redcoat ranks.

On a ridge immediately to the north of where the MacDonald regiments waited a group of schoolboys lay in the heather, watching intently as history unfurled below them. Wrapped in their plaids, they had been out all night. Archibald Fraser was nine and the youngest son of Simon Fraser, Lord Lovat and the chief of the name. The boys searched the battle lines for their clans, but Lovat was never to arrive in time with his reinforcements. However, James Mackintosh did see his father, Angus Mackintosh of Farr, march onto the moor at the head of a company in the Clan Chattan regiment. They passed close to where Archibald, James and their friends lay, but the children were so awed and terrified that they did not dare call out or stand up. Although he lived to be 90, James never forgot the look on his father's face.

At around one o'clock in the afternoon the war pipes were stilled for a moment as the first volley of cannon fire erupted over the moor.

Government artillery was immeasurably more effective and round shot began to tear into the groups of clansmen. Gunners aimed low and hoped that their cannonballs would ricochet off the ground, like flat stones skimming over water, before ploughing through the enemy ranks. It proved a murderous tactic, killing scores of men, maiming more. And it drew a remarkable response.

As their standards fluttered and snapped in the driving rain, the clansmen lifted their broadswords, tightened their grip on their targes and began to summon the army of the dead.

For what they would later call 'Am Bliadhna Thearlaich', the Year of Charles, they had followed the Prince, their ferocious charges sweeping aside government armies, reaching to within three days' march of London. Before they roared their war cries at Prestonpans, at Falkirk and a dozen other skirmishes, before they tore into the terrified redcoats and cut them to pieces, the clansmen had stood quietly in their ranks and remembered who they were and why they had come with the Prince to fight. Many men recited their genealogy: 'Is mise mac Domhnaill, mac Iain, mac Iain Ruadh', I am the son of Donald, the son of John, the son of Red John. Some could go back through their lineage to near-mythic ancestors. Before they raced across the heather at Culloden, they needed to remember them, to summon up all of the memory of their people, all of their ancient prowess, to come to the moor to fight beside them.

For reasons lost to history Prince Charles had ignored the advice of Lord George Murray, his only talented general, and decided to take personal charge of the army. But he seemed paralysed by poor communication and indecision. As the round shot cut down more and more clansmen, survivors roared at their officers, begging for the 'Claidheamh Mòr'. It never came. Unable to stand the cannon fire any longer, Clan Chattan finally broke away, screaming the names of their places,

LEFT *The Great Sword, the 'Claidheamh Mòr', or claymore.*

'Loch Moy! Dunmaglass!' When they saw the Wildcats race away the Appin Stewarts and the Atholl Brigade raised their broadswords and broke into the charge and Cameron of Locheil led his clans into the gunfire.

The schoolboys in the heather strained to see what was happening through the rain and the smoke. James Mackintosh probably knew that Clan Chattan was away and that his father was leading them, running towards the lines of redcoats, but he could not see him. And he never saw him again.

It was chaos. Clans collided as they avoided boggy ground and the whole line slewed badly to the right. Most of the army on the left, including the powerful MacDonald regiments, never engaged properly and in less than an hour the Prince was being led off the battlefield as he told his officers to save themselves. Charles would spend three months in hiding in the Highlands, sheltered by sympathizers before taking ship for France and a life pondering what might have been.

Murdoch MacLeod disappeared into the smoke, carnage and chaos of Culloden. Nothing more was heard of him. Perhaps he fled, and like some clansmen later changed his name. Or perhaps he is buried in one of the mass graves dug on Drummossie Moor.

Defeat at Culloden was the beginning of a long end for the clans. Within two generations the great emigrations had begun, the working landscape of the Highlands quickly decaying into scenery, the mighty language of the Gael on its way to becoming a lexical curiosity. By the end of the 19th century clan society had all but gone, its memory kept alive by Caledonian societies, sentimental music, tartanry and the extraordinary success of Sir Walter Scott.

The story of Scotland's Highland clans is remarkable, the truth of it as highly coloured and romantic as the fiction. Occupying half of Scotland, a sixth of the land mass of Britain and many of their best having departed for the corners of the earth, the clans made all sorts of history. They won several kingdoms, created a great Atlantic state, made memorable music and poetry, threatened the British constitution more than once and were instrumental in the making of the modern world.

2

At First Light
the Standards Gleamed

 IGH ABOVE THE NEVIS RANGES EAGLES CAN OFTEN BE SEEN HUNTING. Soaring on the updrafts, banking and tilting their wingspreads, they search the ground for movement, a stern gaze alert for even the smallest disturbance in the heather. The great birds live immense lives, some hen-eagles have survived more than a hundred years in captivity, and through the snows and thaws of ten thousand winters their wild cousins have watched the landscape of the Highlands change.

It began with nothingness. The last ice age swept all life from what is now Scotland, creating a pitiless, endless vista of white. Dominated by the ice domes, huge hemispherical mountains of compacted ice, sometimes half a kilometre thick, the Highlands were crushed under their weight. Over the ranges north of Loch Lomond a massive dome formed. Incessant hurricanes blew around its symmetrical slopes, and often the downward flow of wind created sustained periods of anti-cyclone and clear, dazzling blue skies. It was a landscape of devastating beauty.

When the weather began to warm, some time around 11,000 BC, the domes groaned and cracked. Glaciers splintered off and very slowly moved across the face of the land, their edges fraying and melting. Carrying millions of tons of debris inside them, huge boulders and pods of gravel, the glaciers began to bulldoze the landscape of the Highlands into its familiar shape. River courses were scarted out, mountainsides planed and sheared into cliff faces, and as the sea filled and rose it pushed the long fingers of sea-lochs into the heart of Scotland.

By 8000 BC the ice had gone. Within a very short time a green tide of grassland and herbage flowed north, trees grew and animals migrated to graze and browse a vast wildwood. Predators followed. The eagles flew above the mountains once more and from the warmth of the south, pioneers gradually made their way into the virgin landscape.

These people were not primitive but highly skilled and resourceful, living by hunting, fishing and ingathering a wild harvest of fruit, nuts, fungi, roots and salad leaves. As the weather improved more came and more established communities flourished. Archaeologists now believe that the Western and Northern Isles and the Atlantic coastline were patterned by many successful settlements. To ensure a year-round supply of food the shoreline was a good place to live and many modern villages have a long continuity.

When techniques of farming arrived in the extreme north-west of Europe, in around 3000 BC, communities were able to produce surpluses, enough to enable men and women to work on tasks unrelated to food production. The great prehistoric monuments at Calanais on the Isle of Lewis and those on Orkney are the relics of successful economies. DNA studies confirm that this is more than merely interesting. They show that the early farmers of the west are the direct ancestors of the clans, and indeed most people still living in the Highlands today.

The populous prehistoric western seaboard suffered a cataclysm that changed the land forever. Precisely dated to 1159 BC by the analysis of ancient tree ring growth, the Icelandic volcano of Hekla suddenly blew itself apart. It was a stupendous explosion, so loud that the distant thunderous rumble could have been heard in north-west Scotland. Moments later a tsunami raced towards the Hebrides and the mainland at an astonishing 500 kilometres an hour, and when it smashed onshore entire communities were engulfed and trees snapped like matchsticks as it tore inland.

But the giant wave was only a prelude. The eruption of Hekla sent millions of tonnes of ash and debris rocketing high into the atmosphere. The prevailing winds blew the huge ash clouds eastwards, and they accelerated as they became more buoyant. When the clouds reached the Highland and island coastlines a dense black rain fell in the half-darkness. The sun was almost completely screened by a deadly aerosol of condensing water vapour, volcanic dust and sulphuric acid. Vast thunderstorms rent the air as the massive clouds collided over the mountains. Lightning crackled and the sky flashed, boomed and roared. Watchers who cowered in caves must have believed that the gods were at war, that the world was ending in an elemental agony of darkness and foul rain.

For many it did end. The volcanic winter created by the eruption of Hekla lasted a generation. Studies of the sequences of tree rings on ancient Irish oaks which were alive in 1159 BC and the terrible aftermath show negligible growth as the sun was occluded for 18 years. There were no summers, nothing grew and ripened, there were no harvests to gather in. The Western Highlands and islands became a soaking, cold and toxic desert. Once food stores ran out, famine gripped the land with perhaps half of the population perishing. Endless rain fell and sodden vegetation rotted and peat began to blanket the landscape.

When the eagles that had survived the black rain and the storms looked down they saw bands of refugees climbing over the high passes of Drumalban, the mountainous spine of Highland Scotland. After 1159 BC it divided a new and wet Atlantic climate from the drier eastern lands of the North Sea coast. It still does.

Those who remained in the west were forced to change their way of life. As the rain fell and the peat spread, arable farming became more and more difficult and stock rearing was widely adopted. It could be managed with fewer people and under darkening skies hardy cattle and sheep could survive in a damp but green landscape. Good grazing could be found on hillsides where run-off prevented the formation of peat-beds.

Archaeology suggests that society changed with the climate. Finds of many more metal weapons, preserved in the anaerobic wetlands, speak of fearful times, of warriors and conflict, of the need to protect what meagre resources were left after the disaster of Hekla. Highland geography naturally separated communities by land (but linked them by sea and loch) and it is not difficult to imagine the development of self-sufficient kindreds living in settlements strung out along the floors of steep-sided glens or on the offshore islands. Warlords and a warrior elite could guarantee the security of their farmers and herders in return for food renders or service, or even, in extremis, military obligations. These are the foundations of clan society. But similar circumstances existed in many places. What made Highland clan society distinctive was its language, its culture and its longevity.

British Celtic languages are not mutually intelligible; they fall into two clear groups. Welsh, Cornish and Breton (as its name implies, originally a British language) are P-Celtic, while Irish, Scots Gaelic and Manx are Q-Celtic. These handy labels derive from the difference between *map* and *mac* for *son of* or *pen* and *ceann* for *head*, but in reality there are many, far wider differences.

OVERLEAF *The monumental Neolithic stone circle at Calanais on the Isle of Lewis.*

ABOVE *A still winter evening at Loch Maree in the north-west Highlands.*

P-Celtic was spoken over most of Britain when the Roman Empire began to take an interest at the end of the 1st millennium BC. From Caithness to Cornwall military maps made for imperial generals recorded place names in an early form of Old Welsh. Personal names also support this notion. In Ireland and across the North Channel in Argyll (and perhaps further north) Q-Celtic or Gaelic was commonly understood. What later pushed Gaelic northwards and eastwards over Drumalban was the ultimate political success of the Argyll kings. By the 11th century the macMalcolm dynasty ruled over most of Scotland, and by the 13th century the last speech communities who spoke the northern dialects of Old Welsh had died out.

Some of the unwritten stories of the origins of the clans are whispered in the so-called archaisms of the Gaelic language. It describes the colour and nuance of an ancient agricultural life, is meticulous about the weather and its seasons, precise on the moods of the sea and it chronicles the cycle of the pre-Christian year. Stock rearing governed how the Celts of the west calculated their calendar.

Samhuinn signalled the end of summer and the slaughter of fat cattle, their preservation and a feast to celebrate the beginning of a new year. Halloween is the modern name for the day before Samhuinn but its rituals of turnip lanterns, guizing (now Americanized as trick or treat) and the lighting of bonfires (moved a few days later to commemorate the capture of Guy Fawkes) remember the old Celtic way of life. *Oidhche Shamhna* or Samhuinn Eve was the night when the shadow bodies of the dead walked once more among the living, the night when the veil between worlds was gossamer thin. All over Scotland there are Celtic place names that incorporate versions of *teine*, the fire, and, often hilltops or ridges, these were where the new year blazed into life and where the living and the dead danced and sang in the flickering shadows.

At *Imbolc* in late February the first fruits of the spring began to glow. In preparation for lambing ewes began to lactate and there was milk for hungry bellies. May Day was once known as *Beltainn*, literally, the fire of Bel, a Celtic god. It celebrated fertility so overtly and joyfully that the church spent centuries suppressing the Beltane feasts. At Padstow in Cornwall the righteous failed spectacularly and among packed and very merry crowds on May Day the Obby Oss, a man dressed as a stallion, still dances among the crowds to the music of time when he drags young women under the skirted frame of his elaborate costume.

The year ends with *Lughnasa* when the first cuts of hay have been harvested in July and early August and the wild fruits of the woods are ripe. But mainly it is a festival of propitiation, sacrifices and promises made to the capricious and sometimes malevolent gods, encouragements to allow a good harvest in September and October. The Celtic peoples of all Britain once lived in the rhythms of the stock-rearing year and despite the influences of Christianity, Highlanders lived them the longest, until well into the 17th and early 18th centuries.

In the 1670s bulls were still being sacrificed to pagan gods in the Highlands, and the elders of the presbytery of Applecross, on the mainland opposite Skye, complained of 'abominable and heathenish practices'. Apparently men from Achnashellach had gathered in an ancient holy place and carried on certain rituals such as walking *deasail* or sunwise in a circle and then killing a bull in an attempt to propitiate the gods. It was not an isolated incident. In the desperate hope of improving his wife, Cirstane's, health, Hector Mackenzie had ferried a bull across to the sacred island of Eilean Ma Ruibhe in Loch Maree and in the summer of 1678 had it killed and its blood spilled in sacrifice. The god named was *Mourie*. This time it was the turn of Dingwall presbytery to complain. It is striking that, in extremis,

Hector's pagan beliefs ignored almost a thousand years of Christianity. Eilean Ma Ruibhe had been named after the early Christian missionary, St Maelrubai, who sailed from Ireland to convert the Picts in 671. Loch Maree is also named after him, but the island had clearly been sacred to pagans, and when he had his bull poleaxed Hector Mackenzie clearly knew that. And believed in its power.

Cattle were the principal measures of wealth in the 1st millennium BC. Their central place is celebrated in the ancient Irish epic poem, the *Táin Bó Cúailgne*, or the Cattle Raid of Cooley. Only written down in the early medieval period, when it was already very old, the poem reaches back many centuries into prehistory. The action turns on the fate of the Brown Bull of Cooley and the war between the armies of Ulster and Connaught. The hero-warrior is the great young swordsman, Cúchulainn, and he defends Ulster single-handedly against allcomers. Some of the eternal themes of clan society are to be found in the *Táin Bó*: military prowess, chronic cattle raiding and the pursuit and celebration of glory.

The latter was much on the mind of the Roman Emperor Claudius. Dragged onto the imperial throne from behind a curtain by the Praetorian Guard after the calamitous reign of Caligula he needed urgently to transform his image as a stuttering, hesitant, weak and unlikely emperor. Military success or conquest were the usual means and in AD 43 the invasion of Britain began.

It took the Romans 40 years to reach the foot of the Highland massif. When the legionaries marched up the north road under the command of Agricola they had reconnoitred thoroughly and almost certainly sent envoys ahead to attempt to negotiate a peaceful takeover. A bloodless conquest was always cheaper and glorious in its own way. This approach seems to have been successful in Lothian and Fife. The kings of the Votadini and the Venicones (allies known as the Kindred Hounds) had not offered battle but instead agreed to sell their surplus corn to the Roman quartermasters. But the Highlanders, the Caledonians, to the north were different, hostile and probably long-time enemies of the southern British kingdoms. On the Gask Ridge, running from Doune to Perth, the Romans had built a line of forts and watchtowers along what was probably a pre-existing frontier. Immediately to the north place names recall a different territory. Dunkeld means 'Fort of the Caledonians' and rising up behind is Schiehallion, the 'Magic Mountain of the Caledonians'. *Caledonii* itself probably meant 'The Warriors'. Ancient faultlines were emerging.

ABOVE *Calgacus addresses his soldiers before the battle at Mons Graupius in AD 83. Despite the tartan and the harp, the chariot does not look out of place.*

Like the Duke of Cumberland in 1746, Agricola had the good sense to shadow his army offshore with a supporting fleet. Tacitus, the great historian, recorded that the Roman invasion force had reached the Angus glens by the summer of AD 82. At that point the general made an uncharacteristic mistake when he decided not to brigade his legions and auxiliaries into one huge army group. Perhaps he thought it easier for individual legions to forage, perhaps there was localized skirmishing better dealt with by smaller units.

As darkness fell on a late summer's night, somewhere in the shadow of the Grampian Mountains, the Caledonian warlords who watched the

IX Legion light their cooking fires and settle down for the night in their marching camp will have noted that the gateways were heavily guarded, but not blocked by anything solid. The freshly dug ditches and ramparts were also not formidable, able only to slow down an assault but not stop it.

To launch a night attack it is likely that war horns sounded the charge, and out of the shadows the Caledonian warriors raced for the gates, roaring their war cries. 'They cut down the sentries and burst into the sleeping camp, creating panic', wrote Tacitus. With little or no time to buckle on body armour the legionaries grabbed their helmets, shields and weapons and fought back as best they could, blundering among the leather tents and guy ropes. Earlier in the northern campaign the warbands had attacked forts and knew what to expect. It looked as though there would be a great slaughter, and just as three legions had been annihilated in the forests of Germany 70 years before, the IX would be wiped out on the fateful fringes of the Scottish Highlands.

But help came. Perhaps the legate commanding the IX Legion had somehow got gallopers away out of the melee and they had found Agricola's division. Reinforcements arrived in the nick of time and by dawn the warbands had been driven off. Memorably, Tacitus wrote, 'At first light the standards gleamed.'

This is the first notice of the Highland charge, the first time the kindreds who would become the clans raced into recorded history. But it would not be long before a second view of charging Caledonians was seen by Roman legionaries.

The summer after the night attack, in AD 83, the Caledonian confederacy chose their ground for a great battle. At Mons Graupius, somewhere in the north-east, the warbands drew up on sloping ground, probably near where the legions had encamped. The Caledonians were led by a warlord named Calgacus, the first Highlander with any historical personality. His name means 'The Swordsman'. As the two armies faced each other, Tacitus put words in his mouth, words that have echoed down the centuries wherever Highland warriors have mustered. They cannot have been accurate, but they sound authentic. 'On into battle!' shouted Calgacus, 'And as you go think both of your ancestors and your descendants.' The naming, the *sloinneadh*, was therefore an old ritual, and a traditional means of finding courage as the front of battle glowered.

Tacitus mentions no charge, and naturally lays great emphasis on superior Roman discipline and equipment. The long shields and short stabbing swords of the legionaries were designed for the close-quarter fighting first developed by the Greeks in the formation known as the phalanx. Weight of numbers, pushing, hacking and keeping the shield-wall tight was what won battles around the shores of the Mediterranean. Once an enemy took a backward step momentum began and accelerated, and the legionaries would push hard, legs pumping, and quickly turn retreat into rout.

The Caledonian equipment was useless, wrote Tacitus, for this sort of warfare. Their shields were too small, only good for parrying, and their long slashing swords entirely unsuitable in the ruck of close-quarter combat.

These contrasts and observations might as easily have been applied to Culloden, but the Highland charge did not remain unchanged for the 17 centuries separating 1746 and Mons Graupius. It was in fact developed in its modern form in the 1640s, probably first used again by the great MacDonald captain, Alasdair MacColla, in order to deal with musketry and artillery. Once 17th-century Lowland armies had fired their first round and begun the laborious business of reloading what muskets they had, the clansmen charged, claymores raised, racing to reach the enemy line in time. If they did, then the result was never in doubt.

Tacitus' fascinating account of the Scottish campaigns of Agricola is also the first notice of the Highland Line, the most profound cultural (and geological) boundary in Scotland, and probably in Britain. To the south and east the Romans had found agriculturalists who spoke a version of Old Welsh. In the glens and the mountains they found trouble. It was a distinction that did persist for 17 centuries, often flaring into violence. Not until Culloden did that old frontier begin to blur. After 1746 Lowland Scots south of the line ceased to fear the clansmen and increasingly despised and patronized them. What was known as 'miorun mor nan Gall' was born. 'The great malice of the Lowlander' lasted many centuries.

K. Robert Bruce began his Raigne 1306

Isabel daughter Earl of Marr

3

OUT OF THE MOUTH
OF THE MORNING

NXIOUS TO LEGITIMIZE HIS CLAIMS TO THE THRONE OF
SCOTLAND, Robert the Bruce commissioned the brilliant
cleric, Bernard de Linton, to send a formal letter to the pope in
1321. It has become known as the Declaration of Arbroath,
famous for its stirring words: 'so long as one hundred of us remain alive we
shall never surrender to the domination of the English'. For the sake of
medieval historical form, de Linton prefaced the politics with a fancy origin
legend for the Scottish people. Every self-respecting nation needed one, but
the opening of the Declaration has since been dismissed as myth-history.
It speaks of an epic voyage from the Eastern Mediterranean to the Straits of
Gibraltar and beyond:

> *The which Scottish nation, journeying from Greater Scythia by the Tyrrhene
> Sea and the Pillars of Hercules, could not in any place or time or manner be
> overcome by the barbarians, though long dwelling in Spain among the fiercest
> of them. Coming thence, 1,200 years after the transit of Israel, with many
> victories and many toils they won that habitation in the west, which though
> the Britons have been driven out, the Picts effaced, and the Norwegians,
> Danes and English have often assailed it, they hold now, in freedom from all
> vassalage: and as the old historians bear witness, have ever so held it. In this
> kingdom have reigned 113 kings of their own Blood Royal, and no man
> foreign has been among them.*

No part of this fascinating passage was a figment of de Linton's imagination for it described how Gaelic-speaking Scotland saw its beginnings. And
now it turns out that this Homeric journey may be more than a tradition.
Recent DNA studies along the Atlantic seaboard of Scotland have discovered
markers that originated in the Near East and in Spain and Portugal. These
suggest traces of a long migration, and since they also show continuity over

ABOVE *The Declaration of Arbroath, 1321, with the seals of Scotland's nobility attached.*

PRECEDING PAGES *Sporting a splendid moustache, King Robert the Bruce poses with his first wife, Isabella of Mar, herself a heraldic marvel.*

millennia in the Hebrides and on the western coasts, it may be the case that elements of the western clans have exotic origins.

Recent scholarship supports the notion of migration from the south to Ireland and western Scotland, or at least the transfer of language and the cultural habits bound up in it. Celtic languages were probably carried to north-west Europe in boats, passed on by traders and what is called enclave colonization. In the 1st millennium BC, and possibly before, goods regularly passed up the Atlantic seaboard from Cadiz in southern Spain to Galicia,

Biscay, Britanny, Ireland and western Scotland. Archaeology confirms these links and makes a strong case that the Irish and Scots Gaelic languages came from the south.

Seeing the sea as a highway rather than a barrier encourages the idea of a Gaelic-speaking culture developing on both sides of the North Channel at around the same time. But it is not dramatic, a process rather than a story, and that prosaic version of history does not appeal to clerics compiling a list of kings, 113 of them, of the Blood Royal. De Linton needed a figurehead and in Fergus macEirc he found one.

Fergus was the traditional progenitor, the first name in that long genealogy of native Scottish kings and it is thought that he lived around the year AD 500. His kingdom spanned the North Channel; Dalriada incorporating territory in Antrim and Argyll. It was a Gaelic-speaking kingdom and Argyll means 'the Coastlands of the Gael'. Old geography applies the name to all of the seaboard between Kintyre and Loch Broom, but more usually it describes the lands between the Firth of Lorne and the Mull of Kintyre.

Fergus ruled over three kindreds. The Cenél Loairn held the area north of Loch Fyne and has left its name on the map as Lorne. To the west the Cenél nOengusa controlled the fertile island of Islay and to the east the largest kindred, the Cenél nGabrain, settled Kintyre, Knapdale and some of the smaller offshore islands. The Cenél Comhghall later claimed a fourth group and named the Cowal peninsula.

At least one of these kindreds was composed of smaller but distinct units whose structure seems closer to a later sense of clanship. Like Clan Chattan, they appear to have formed an alliance. The Cenél Loairn comprised the Cenél Fergus, the Cenél Cathbad and the Cenél nEachach. These personal names may remember warlords, for there is no doubt that the kindreds were thought of as military entities.

A surprising survival, giving what sound like accurate numbers in an age of chronic vagueness, the *Senchus Fer nAlban* (The History of the Men of Scotland), is essentially a muster roll. It lists each kindred and their naval strength. The Argyll kings sailed to war, and their muster was reckoned in boat loads of warriors. Cenél nGabrain was the largest and could launch 70 small ships carrying almost 1,000 marines. Even 1,200 years before Prestonpans, Falkirk and Culloden the military strength of the peoples of the west was formidable.

Fergus macEirc was remembered as an Irish prince who came across the water to Scotland and there is an unmistakably Irish atmosphere around

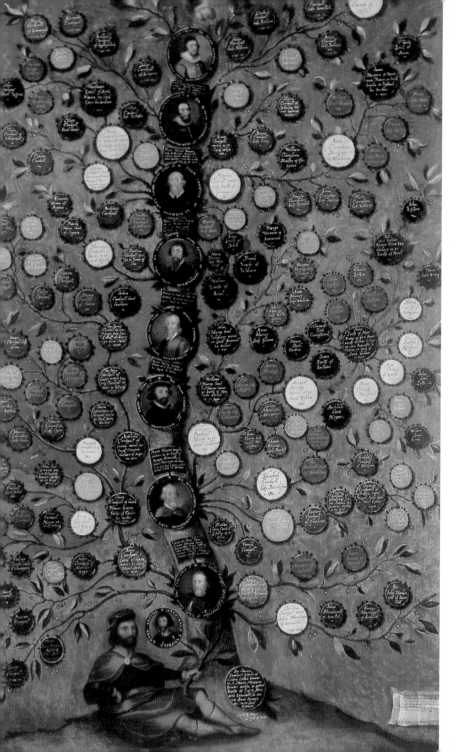

the origin stories of a few of the clans of the south-west. Bards sang of these tales as coming 'out of the mouth of the morning'.

Clan Donald claimed descent from the ancient Irish king Conn of the Hundred Battles or sometimes opted for links with the mythical boy-hero, Cúchulainn. The confederacy that evolved from the Cenél Comhghall and controlled the Cowal peninsula, Lamonts, MacNeills, MacLachlans and MacLays, believed that their genealogy began with Niall of the Nine Hostages, High King of Ireland. Clan Campbell, the most powerful and ambitious in the south-west after the medieval period, insisted that they came from another Irish hero, Diarmaid the Boar. It is an interesting fiction for it is much more likely that the Campbells developed out of the Old Welsh speaking kindreds around the Firth of Clyde. The derivation of their name hints that they may not originally have spoken Gaelic: Campbell means 'twisted mouth'.

As early as the 6th century Gaels did not understand Old Welsh speakers and there exists a clear example of non-comprehension. When Columba came from Ireland to found his monastery on Iona he saw the conversion of the Picts as part of his mission. Their kings ruled over most of the northern and eastern Highlands. When the Gaelic-speaking Columba appeared at the court of King Bridei, somewhere near Inverness, he needed an interpreter.

As the Argyll kings pushed eastwards and, in the language of the Declaration of Arbroath, Pictish political power was effaced, Gaelic began to spread. It was the language of power, increasingly the language of a successful elite. By 900 Constantine II, King of Scotland, was using the Gaelic name for his country when he called it *Alba*. The axis of the kingdom had shifted eastwards from Dalriada to Perthshire and Fife, to Scone and St Andrews. But identity did not equate to unity or tranquillity. After his long reign (900 to 943) Constantine's throne was fought over by rival candidates for more than 150 years. One of the more successful was King MacBeth who ruled between 1040 and 1057. He was able to establish sufficient authority to risk a long absence on pilgrimage to Rome in 1050 where 'he scattered money like seed'.

Against the background of shifting and patchy royal control, local war-lords became leaders of kinship groups and clan territories began to evolve.

OPPOSITE *The family tree of the Campbells of Glenorchy, 1635.*

With a warrior elite at his back, a warlord/chief could not only offer military leadership but could also act as a law-giver and judge. The Highland geography of glens, sea-lochs and confined coastal flatlands encouraged local political development of this sort, but its growth was another quiet process, not an event of great drama which might catch the eye of chroniclers.

A man who did light up the shores of the west, like a lightning storm, emerged in the middle of the 12th century. Undoubtedly charismatic, possessed of great military dash and utterly ruthless, Somerled the Viking made himself the first Lord of the Isles. Clan Donald historians recorded his origins as both Irish and royal, and his emergence as a reclamation of what was rightfully his. It was a familiar device used to legitimize and dignify naked power politics. Despite being traditionally described as a Viking (his mother was of Scandinavian descent, and his name is from *Sumar-lidi*, Norse for Summer Raider), Somerled began to clear the Norse sea-lords out of the southern isles and the mainland. By 1140 he had Knapdale, Lorne, Argyll and Kintyre in his grip, what was ancient Dalriada, and later he seized the kingdom of Man and all the northern Hebrides. It was a vast Atlantic principality.

Somerled sailed into history. Clearly he was a great admiral and an innovator: his *naibheagan*, the small ships, were highly manoeuvrable, able to run rings around the longships of his enemies. His shipwrights had fitted hinged rudders, whereas the longboats used a much slower steering oar. It was called a *steerboard* and is the origin of the term *starboard*. When his sailors captured Islay, Somerled made it his base and called his fortress *Dunyvaig*, the 'Fort of the Small Ships'.

In 1164 the great Lord of the Isles fatally overreached himself, challenging for the throne of all Scotland. Malcolm IV met the army of the Isles at Renfrew, near Glasgow, but the great Gaelic prince was betrayed, stabbed to death in his tent by a kinsman. The heart torn out of them, Somerled's soldiers pushed their galleys out into the Clyde and set sail for the west and their Hebridean homelands. The lordship was divided between Somerled's sons, Ranald, Dugall and Ruari. Their heirs became Clan Ranald, the MacDougalls and the MacRuaris.

By the time of the Wars of Independence in the early 14th century, the MacDonald descendants of Clan Ranald chose wisely and fought with Robert the Bruce at Bannockburn. Swinging their Lochaber axes, the clansmen shouted 'Clann Domhnaill!' and plunged into the crush of mounted English knights. The Islesmen made a great slaughter that day, climbing over

ABOVE *The arms of the Lords of the Isles in the 16th century, with a birlinn at the centre.*

the wrack of dead horses and screaming, dying men, forcing Edward II's great army backwards until it broke and ran.

The MacDougalls had made the mistake of opposing Robert the Bruce and after the MacDonald heroics at Bannockburn, their lands were forfeit and they passed to Angus Og MacDonald, the chief of the name. In 1346 the

last chief of the MacRuaris died, and the male line died with him. His sister, Amie, married John MacDonald of Islay and her lands of Garmoran, the coastline and the islands between Ardnamurchan and Skye passed back into the lordship. Somerled's great dominion was at last reformed. After only the kings of England and Scotland the Lords of the Isles were the greatest landowners in Britain.

As the lordship prospered, famous names emerged. At the Council of the Isles that met at Finlaggan on Islay four great men of royal Clan Donald blood attended. They were the chiefs of Clanranald, MacIain of Ardnamurchan, MacDonald of Kintyre and MacDonald of Keppoch. Their direct descendants led the MacDonald regiments at Culloden. Four powerful chiefs also came: MacLean of Duart, MacLaine of Loch Buie, MacLeod of Harris and MacLeod of Lewis, and they were joined by four *thanes*, MacKinnon, MacNeill of Barra, MacNeill of Gigha and one other magnate who may have taken his seat by rotation. The Bishop of the Isles and the Abbot of Iona, both of them almost always aristocrats, were also members.

Policy and war were discussed at Finlaggan, and matters of state. The law was administered by hereditary judges known as *brieves*, and they knew the codes by heart and precedent, custom and practice and all their nuances were absorbed and handed down. The underlying theme of Celtic law was punishment by reparation (fines or services imposed) rather than judicial revenge, the cutting off of hands or heads, as happened in the Anglo-Norman south. And there was an accepted tariff of fines for specific offences. For an oral tradition, the laws of the Celtic west could go into dizzying detail. On the subject of bees, the husbanding of swarms and the location of hives, for example, a brieve had a great deal to say.

ABOVE *The effigy of Bricius MacKinnon, 14th century.*

OPPOSITE *The Battle of Bannockburn from the Holkham Bible Picture Book, 1327.*

The Highlands and islands of the west prospered under the lordship: Tiree was seen as a lucrative granary and the annual agricultural output of Islay was prodigious. The MacDonalds and their allies grew wealthy and powerful, and parts of their elusive legacy can be glimpsed on the shores of their great principality. Above all the Lords of the Isles were sea-kings and their castles and strongholds are all strategically placed on promontories that command the highways of the sea and are adjacent to sheltered bays where boats might be safely beached.

Many of the sea-castles are beautiful, lonely and not easily reached by road. Around the shores of the Firth of Lorn and the Sound of Mull, a network of strongholds stood in sight of each other. Castle Duart, on a promontory of the MacLean lands in southern Mull, can be seen from Dunstaffnage on the mainland near Oban, and from its towers the squat, immensely thick walls of Ardtornish are visible. No road leads to Ardtornish and the many who came there in the Middle Ages disembarked from ships beached in the sheltered bay below the castle mount. On either shore of the Ardnamurchan peninsula lie Mingary Castle and, to the north, perhaps the most atmospheric and monumental of them all, Castle Tioram.

The small ships sailed so brilliantly by Somerled and his captains developed into the Hebridean birlinn, a beautiful craft. Wooden, slim and shallow-draughted, it could run before a freshening wind with astonishing speed. And when the need for stealth or flight dictated, the birlinn could slide over shallow and rocky water without scraping or fouling its keel. A Gaelic poem of 1310 catches the confidence their navy gave the Lords of the Isles:

> Tall men are arraying the fleet, which swiftly holds its course on the sea's bare surface: no hand lacks a trim warspear, in battle of targes, polished and comely... They have a straight stern wind behind them...their dappled sails are bulging, foam rises to the vessels' sides.

Prosperity was also promoted by a canny policy of exporting potential trouble. Young warriors with too little to do in times of relative peace can often be an incendiary element. The Lords of the Isles and their chiefs encouraged their young men to become mercenaries in the interminable wars between medieval Irish kings. From the Gaelic Gall-Óglaigh, or foreign warriors, these men formed companies of what became known as Gallowglasses.

Their strategic value was immense, but far from using the charge, they were employed to repel it. The Irish kings needed to be able to counter representatives of one of the most powerful military elites in medieval Europe, the armoured Anglo-Norman knight fighting on horseback. The Gallowglasses obliged. Wearing iron helmets, a thick chain-mail shirt known

ABOVE *The dramatic MacLean castle at Duart on the Isle of Mull, by Paul Sandby, 1748.*

as a jack, which reached down to their knees, they formed tight ranks that could withstand charging armoured knights. The stout mail shirt gave confidence (jackboots protected their legs, and a shortened shirt was known as a jacket) and the Highland companies were famously disciplined. In the 1500s an English soldier, Sir Anthony St Leger, noted:

> *These sort of men be those that do not lightly abandon the field, but bide the brunt to the death.*

Gallowglasses became much sought-after, and not only by Irish kings. In 1494 Charles VIII of France invaded Italy and took the city of Florence without a fight but insisted on a triumphal entry for his conquering mercenary army. A horrified Florentine wrote in his diary:

> The heavy cavalry presented a hideous appearance, with their horses looking like monsters because their manes and tails were cut quite short. Then came the archers, and then extraordinary tall men from Scotland and other northern countries, and they looked more like wild beasts than men.

Military success in Ireland and elsewhere not only underwrote tranquility in the lordship, but it also encouraged emigration. Grateful kings sometimes endowed Gallowglasses with grants of land as well as payment in gold and silver, and there are now many MacDonalds, MacDonnells and MacSweens in Ulster. The bonds of Dalriada were never completely severed.

History caught up once more when the Lords of the Isles over-reached themselves a second time. In 1462 John of Islay and King Edward IV of England signed the Treaty of Westminster-Ardtornish (the sea-castle on the Morvern shore), and its terms seem now to be breathtaking. If the boy-king, James III of Scotland, could be deposed then Edward and the Lord of the Isles would divide his kingdom between them. What brings this apparent hubris sharply into a contemporary context is the fact that on his accession at Ardtornish John of Islay could muster 10,000 soldiers and 250 birlinns. The treaty was no pipe dream, but it did prove fatal. When the details of John's agreement with the English – and what was seen as his treachery – were discovered James III forced him to forfeit his great estates, and in 1493 he became a captive pensioner at the royal household. The lordship began to disintegrate and within three generations it had become a patchwork of clan territories.

Few of the achievements of the old principality survived so impressively or for so long as the Great Music. Coming on record in 1580, the piping college of the MacCrimmons had been established much earlier. The *Ceol Mor*, the Great Music of the Highland bagpipes, has endured as a classical canon of about 300 pieces. These are stately melodies: laments, gatherings or salutes, and they contrast with the *Ceol Beag*, the lesser music of slow airs, jigs and marches.

Bagpipes are unique, different from other wind instruments. Best heard outdoors, they are mouth-blown through a reed that thrives on being dampened by saliva and played almost every day to keep its condition stable. Because the chanter, which allows notes to be played, is fixed below the bag there can be no loud/soft variation and this calls for singular skills from

OPPOSITE *Painted in 1714, this early portrait of the piper to the chiefs of Clan Grant carried their banner and motto, and shows the chiefs' stronghold in the background.*

ABOVE *Highlanders who fought as mercenaries in early 17th-century Europe. Two archers and a musketeer, all clothed in tartan and some with bare feet, look more apprehensive than fearsome.*

players and composers. Through the single bass drone and the two tenors there is a continuous sound and to bring these into harmony pipers often play a series of informal preludes before they begin the *Ceol Mor*.

Composers (almost all are skilled pipers) use a classical structure developed by the MacCrimmons. First an *urlar*, literally a ground, is laid down and then followed by a series of variations. The climax of the piece is the *crunlath*, where the melody is restated and grace notes added. Perhaps the most readily available sense of what this structure sounds like is a melody most often sung now. The hymn *Amazing Grace* is set to a simple pipe tune and it grows more complex and more beautiful as it is hung with grace notes.

Bagpipe music carries well on a windless day, and Highland armies were not only led into battle by pipers (as were 20th-century Highland regiments), their commanders also used them like buglers. Pipers sounded charges, halts and, rarely, retreats. Confusion threatened to overtake the Jacobite army at Falkirk in 1746 when its pipers gave their instruments to their servants before going in with their claymores. Their cause disappeared into history, but their Great Music has survived, and for a Scot there are few sounds more evocative than the pipes.

4

THE AGE OF THE FORAYS

N 1396 GRANDSTANDS WERE BUILT ON THE RIVER ISLAND KNOWN AS THE NORTH INCH. King Robert III of Scotland, his court and many English and French noblemen had arrived in Perth to watch what promised to be a memorable spectacle. It was not a tournament or horse racing. Two groups of Highland clansmen would fight to the death in a judicial trial by combat, something that had not been seen in Britain for many generations. It is thought that there had been a long-standing dispute over territory between Clan Cameron and Clan Chattan and that all peaceful, legal means of resolution had been exhausted.

Each clan had chosen thirty warriors and they had come to Perth to settle matters by the spilling of blood. No armour, helmets or shields were permitted, and as they formed lines and glared at each other across the grass arena each clansman held a broadsword, a double-bladed Lochaber axe, a dirk, a crossbow and three bolts. As the crowd bayed for blood, screaming encouragements to slaughter, one man lost his nerve, plunged into the Tay and swam back to sanity.

Once a replacement had been found, each clan fired three volleys of crossbow bolts at close range. Many men fell, but most were wounded, some fatally, bleeding to death on the grass, moaning pitifully in their death-agonies – until Clan Chattan began to gain the upper hand in the close-quarter fighting. The crowd roared approval as the Cameron wounded were hacked to pieces as they lay on the ground, blood spurting from vicious cuts. Eventually ten men from Clan Chattan were left standing and only two from Clan Cameron when a halt was called and a verdict declared. In a brief frenzy of butchery, 38 Highlanders had fought and killed each other for the entertainment of packed grandstands and pavilions.

Virtually every British chronicler reported what became known as the Battle of the Clans of 1396. It was as though the barbarities of the Colosseum had been revived, but in reality the grisly event was emblematic of a set of attitudes. Lowland Scotland thought of the clansmen on the North Inch as little more than sub-human savages whose lives were cheap and whose death made suitable sport.

Like all prejudices it begins to unravel on closer examination. The most notorious Highland chief was the feral Wolf of Badenoch. By 1382 he had acquired a wide landholding on the southern shores of the Moray Firth and in Buchan and Badenoch. His most powerful neighbour was the Bishop of Moray, who in 1390 made the great mistake of condemning the Wolf for living in sin, in an adulterous relationship with Máiréad, the daughter of Eachann of Strathnaver. Badenoch's men descended on the bishop's town of Forres and burned it, and then destroyed his cathedral at Elgin. It was an appalling example of Highland savagery, thundered the Church. Except that it was not. The Wolf of Badenoch was also known as Alexander Stewart, and was none other than the brother of King Robert III, the descendant of a famous Norman-French family that had settled in Scotland, and a spectator at the North Inch in Perth. Stewart was no Gael and no clansman.

The Wolf of Badenoch was not the only nobleman to go native in the medieval period. After 1066 the Gaelic-speaking macMalcolm dynasty was increasingly drawn into the Norman-French orbit of England's new regime. Many men whose ancestors originated in Normandy or Northern France came north and over time they were absorbed into clan society. Their names now sound quintessentially Scottish. Bruce and Stewart are the most famous: the former is from the Cotentin Peninsula in north-western France and the latter probably from Brittany. Stewart derived from the role of the ancestors of Walter the Steward, the High Steward of Scotland in the early 14th century. Almost a hundred years earlier, Sir Laurence le Grand became sheriff of Inverness, appointed by Alexander II. Like the MacDonalds, this family chose the successful contender for the Scottish throne in the Wars of Independence and Robert the Bruce rewarded them with extensive lands in Strathspey. By the 15th century the Grants had become powerful, Gaelic-speaking clan chiefs. Mesnières in Normandy is the origin of the difficulty of pronouncing Menzies (most say *Ming-is*, some say *Mean-is*) and after 1249 Sir Robert de Meyneris established his family in Atholl and Glenlyon. In the rising of 1745 the clan came out in force.

ABOVE *A crofting township of blackhouses on the Isle of Barra.*

Sir Robert's descendants did not have the same relationship with their clansmen as English barons had with those who worked their lands. In the Highlands there was markedly less servility. In 1724 General Wade noticed:

> [clansmen] are treated by their Chiefs with great familiarity. They partake with them in their diversions and shake them by the hand wherever they meet them.

Especially in larger and more dispersed clans, chiefs delegated a great deal to tacksmen. They were usually relatives, *daoine uaisle*, or gentry, and they dealt directly with the management of farmland and pasture. Clansmen and their families lived in small clusters of houses known as a *clachan*. Mostly built in drystone around A-frames at the gables and with a turf roof supported by a ridge beam and purlins, these houses became known as blackhouses. Since windows were rare or tiny, doors usually closed and the only light came from a central fire, the down-hearth, the name was attached for obvious reasons. Most blackhouses had a floor of beaten earth with flat stones in the doorway to keep mud to a minimum.

The peat-burning down-hearth sent smoke into the roof where it could seep through a smoke-hole, or if thatch and brackens had been used instead of turf, it may just have seeped. Sparks did not fly up and set the roof alight because of a layer of carbon monoxide which accumulated immediately

ABOVE *Sheiling, a hut used by those tending animals in the hills, on the Isle of Lewis.*

OPPOSITE *Highland women carrying creels of bracken, useful for both roofing and flooring, Hebrides, c. 1880.*

under the roof, and any rudimentary furniture was always low and short-legged to ensure that those sitting around the fire stayed below the haze of smoke and poisonous fumes. Blackhouses were basic to be sure, but snug in a winter storm.

Tacksmen took central roles in clan society. Around each clachan or township lay the inbye rigs. These were long and narrow crested ridges with shallow drainage ditches on either side, and they were used to grow cereals. Some rigs had better soil, better drainage or a better position, and tacksmen allocated them to clansmen on a rotating yearly basis. The system was known as runrig.

Beyond the inbye was the common grazing and the moor where peats and brackens were cut, and these were also overseen by the tacksmen. Beasts had to be kept off the rigs and their growing crops in spring and summer and then brought inbye in the winter to drop their nourishing muck, the only source of fertiliser.

In springtime clansmen undertook the ancient journey of transhumance, driving their black cattle and sheep up the hill trails to the high pastures and the shielings. These were temporary huts and in the light northern nights they were where herdsmen (often women and children) summered out with their animals in the mountains. In Gaelic the shielings were known as summertowns and the clachans as wintertowns. Around the cooking fires in the high pasture tales were told, songs sung and away from the older people, understandings exchanged.

War was the other business delegated to tacksmen. The clans owed their chiefs military service and when the tacksman called men to arms, they were compelled to follow. The fiery cross was lit, a blood-soaked rag attached, and it passed from clachan to clachan as the signal for clansmen to sharpen their claymores and dirks. Not every clansman was anxious to fight, and tacksmen sometimes had to threaten and cajole. In 1812 in Canada the fiery cross was lit one last time to summon the exiled Glengarry Highlanders to oppose a force of invading Americans.

This dramatic symbol reappeared in the southern states of the USA in the 20th century. The most infamous clan of all, the Ku Klux Klan, planted fiery crosses wherever they wished to intimidate.

Medieval Scottish kings recognized the clans as potent social entities and took trouble to empower chiefs so that they could govern them effectively. They were made *hereditary justiciars* and could hand down sentences to those convicted, including the death penalty. Despite the apparent despotism, the bonds of loyalty were old and not often broken. In 1720 an English officer stationed in the Highlands observed:

> *The ordinary Highlanders esteem it the most sublime degree of virtue to love their Chief and pay him a blind obedience though it be in opposition to the government.*

The growing power of the chiefs and their clans was a direct result of the disintegration of the Lordship of the Isles after 1500. Based in the Lowlands, Scottish kings could not hope to exert the same sort of control as the men who ruled from Finlaggan. Their birlinns could reach trouble very quickly and deal with it. Increasingly, clans fought among themselves and disorder reached such a pitch that the 16th century was labelled *Linn nan Creach*, the Age of the Forays.

In the same period central royal government in Scotland was generally weak and even weaker in outlying areas in virtually every compass direction. The 16th century saw the zenith of border reiving, a time when the will of the great riding families was of far more immediate impact than any directives from Edinburgh or the royal court. The Highlands saw similar levels of lawlessness and had the same disregard for distant authority. Occasionally kings ventured north with a large force of heavily armed men, and summary justice was handed down. But sometimes the king's justice caused more problems than it solved.

In 1540 James V was in the Highlands, and along with other chiefs, John of Moidart, Chief of Clan Ranald, was imprisoned. In his enforced absence, the succession was no simple matter of turning to his eldest son or a close relative, as was the habit in the south. Primogeniture was not how one clan chief followed another. The ancient Celtic law of tanistry allowed an old or ailing chief to have a much wider choice and thereby ensure that competent and courageous men took his place. Tanistry made eligible the offspring of the chief's great grandfather and all their descendants, and that meant that even very distant cousins could succeed. It was a mechanism that made for continuity and internal stability.

With John of Moidart in prison, Ranald Gallda installed himself as Chief of Clan Ranald, although he needed the support of Clan Fraser. His close links with them came out of another singular tradition. The children of chiefs were often fostered out to the families of tacksmen or other high-born relatives, and in turn their children came to a chief's house for their upbringing. The Gaelic word *altrum* carries connotations of nursing, educating and caring. Fosterage forged strong bonds of loyalty inside clans and occasionally between different names. Ranald Gallda was able to call on Lord Lovat and the warriors of the Frasers to support his claim to Clan Ranald because he had been fostered in his household.

Chickens were his undoing. Clan chiefs were expected to be open-handed, generous and in a translation of a Gaelic phrase, 'a river to their people'. When Ranald saw cattle being slaughtered for the feast for his inauguration, he is said to have commented that chickens would have done as well. From that day he was known as Ranald of the Chickens.

More seriously, John of Moidart escaped from prison and made his way back to the lands of Clan Ranald in 1543. Ranald fled to his Fraser supporters. The fiery cross was lit and passed along the Great Glen and around the wild and remote area called the Rough Bounds of Moidart. The clans mustered.

John moved first. With Clan Cameron and the MacDonalds of Glengarry, Keppoch and Ardnamurchan, he raided Fraser and Clan Grant lands and took Castle Urquhart on the shores of Loch Ness. Before retaliation could reach him John of Moidart hurried back down the Great Glen and with his men and their loot disappeared into the Rough Bounds. It was as though he had slammed a door behind him. Mountainous country between Loch Sunart and Loch Huorn, the Bounds are perfect for ambush and surprise attack, and no place for captains unfamiliar with its maze of glens, ravines, bogs, lochans and sea-lochs. The Frasers and the Grants resisted the temptation to pursue Clan Ranald into their own territory, and they turned back for home.

Which is exactly what John of Moidart expected. Keeping his men well out of sight, he shadowed the retreat as far as the mouth of Glen Spean, not far up the Great Glen from Fort William. There the small army divided, the Grants taking the Laggan road eastwards towards the Cairngorms and Badenoch, which is exactly what John of Moidart expected. It was then he put his plan into action. Moving rapidly and expertly along the mountain

ABOVE *Woodcut depicting the Chief of the Mac Sweynes at dinner, entertained by a bard and a harpist, c.1578.*

paths, the men of Clan Ranald raced ahead of the Frasers and where the road to Inverness crosses the glen between Loch Lochy and Loch Oich, they waited.

It was a vicious and bloody fight. The two clans clashed in mid-July 1544 and, because of the heat, they are said to have stripped off their coats of mail and their plaids and fought in their shirts. *Blar na Leine*, the Field of the Shirts, was the name given to the battlefield between the lochs. Perhaps the lack of body armour is the reason why it was so bloody. Hundreds were killed, including Lord Lovat and Ranald Gallda. By the evening more of Clan Ranald were left standing and John of Moidart was again undisputed chief.

In September 1544, after news of the battle had found its way south, John was summoned to appear before the Scottish Parliament to answer charges of treason. Safe in the wilds of the Rough Bounds, he ignored the indictment. Ten years later an exasperated question was asked in Edinburgh: 'by what means may all of Scotland be brought to universal obedience and how may John of Moidart be daunted?' How indeed? The Chief of Clan Ranald, like most of his peers, was king in his own small kingdom. Undaunted, he died in his bed in 1584.

Bards flourish on drama, heroes and great battles and there was no lack in the Age of the Forays. As the composers of songs and the keepers of clan history, bards believed that with the resumption of widespread raiding, the

Highlands and islands again resembled the heroic age of Ireland, the events of the tales of Cúchulainn and the Fenian Cycle. But among the nostalgia and the self-conscious archaisms, there are nuggets that show remarkable survivals. It seems that ancient traditions died very hard among the clans. A famous song, *Ic Iain 'Ic Sheumais* commemorates a battle at Carinish in North Uist where a MacDonald warband defeated the MacLeods in 1601. It contains a fascinating passage. A MacDonald warrior lies bleeding in the arms of a woman who sings:

> *Your noble body's blood*
> *Lay on the surface of the ground.*
> *Your fragrant body's blood*
> *Seeped through the linen.*
> *I sucked it up*
> *Till my breath grew husky.*

This was not an isolated example. The Elizabethan poet, Edmund Spenser, was in Ireland only 20 years before Carinish and at the executions of Irish Gaelic rebel leaders, he also witnessed blood drinking. It appears to have been a means of taking in some of the spirit of a great warrior and preserving it in the body of a woman so that it might be passed on.

Not all the traditions of clanship were martial, or gory. Some were a matter of fundamental contention. Chiefs and their clansmen saw the land they lived on in different ways. Language is instructive. Clan is from *clann*, meaning children and there is some sense of this in the way that clansmen – and women – shared a common name. *Mac* is widely understood as *son of* but fewer realize that women should not use it, and instead place *nic* for *daughter of* before their surnames: like a family.

For ordinary clansmen and women, this collective sense of the land they occupied and all of their history together was wrapped up in the idea of *dùthchas*. It does not translate well, but an approximate meaning links a place of birth with a wider heritage and a spirit different from other people and other places. More practically, dùthchas also stood for history, for the right of clansmen to settle and farm the land over which the chiefs and tacksmen provided protection, and where they administered justice. These ancient ideas therefore underwrote a chief's authority because a strong element of collective consent was involved.

The medieval habit of kings granting charters to magnates in the south and chiefs in the north encouraged another way of understanding clan lands.

Oigreachd means heritage, literally, that which is inherited, and for the chiefs the right of their family to own clan lands. Conferred by the king, this version of their rights became more and more powerful. Tanistry began to wane and the rights of chiefs' sons were given much more weight. By the time of Culloden, primogeniture had become the norm – but what gave the charging clansmen their raw courage was the memory of dùthchas. Their war cries were the names of their places because they found it impossible to divide a clan from its ancestral land. When the emigrations of the 19th century gathered pace and people were cleared off the land, often by absentee chiefs, a phenomenon known as *iondrainn* was observed. As the ships sailed further west and out of the sight of land, clansmen and women were overcome with the sense that something was missing, had been removed, and a great sadness descended.

5

THE CLANS DAUNTED

S A BITTER WIND BLEW OFF THE SEA AND UP THE HIGH STREET OF EDINBURGH, Neil MacLeod shivered in his white sark. It was 3 April 1613, the appointed day, and over the heads of the huge crowd gathered at the foot of the gallows, MacLeod looked for the rider who would surely come clattering over the cobbles, shouting, waving the piece of paper in the air. After all that had happened, all he had given up, Holyrood would not abandon him, and the king's reprieve would surely come, even at this hour.

'Come on Bhodach!' hissed one of the executioners, 'We haven't got all bloody day.' MacLeod understood no English and all he heard was the Gaelic word, *bodach*, old man. Full of indignation, he turned and roared, 'Nam bithin air deck luinge far am bu duilich do fhear seasamh, stiuireadh na mara gu tric, cha bhodach dhuit mis' a mhacain!' (If I was on the deck of a ship, steering over the billows, trying to stand steady, you would not call me an old man!) With his hands tied behind his back, MacLeod headbutted the young upstart and knocked him down. The crowd gasped for a moment, and then began to shout insults, baying at the uncomprehending MacLeod that he would soon dance a jig at the end of a rope, soiling himself like a bairn.

As the abuse rose to a crescendo, the chief of the MacLeods of Lewis realized that he was lost, and more, that his death would not be quick. No coin had been handed to the hangman for an easy despatch. No hangers-on would pull at his legs to put him out of his agony. As the noose was looped over his head and pulled savagely tight there was no merciful trapdoor beneath his feet and no hood to blot out the world. With the Edinburgh crowd baying for a good and grisly show, MacLeod was manhandled under a high cross-beam and the rope slung up and over it. When it was taut, the gallowsmen pulled hard and lifted the choking, retching man clean off his feet. Right enough, MacLeod soiled himself and as they winched him almost to the height of the beam, he lost consciousness. And then, suddenly, the gallowsmen let go and he crashed down onto the planking of the platform. Buckets of icy water revived the half-dead MacLeod and he was dragged over to the axeman's block. The screaming crowd hushed as the men held him down, their feet on his back, and the axe was raised high.

The long road to an Edinburgh scaffold had begun almost twenty years before. As it became clearer with every passing year that Elizabeth I of England would bear no children and her heir would be James of Scotland, appearances began to matter very much. And if James was to succeed as King of England, then it was vital that he appeared to be in control of his own kingdom. The Highlands and Islands and their ungovernable clans and arrogant clan chiefs had to be tamed, and the king and his council were determined.

In 1597 the Edinburgh parliament passed an act to enable the foundation of three new towns in the north and west. Clan society was entirely rural and might literally be civilized if towns could be planted in the midst of all that barbarity. There was to be one in Kintyre, another in Lochaber and a third on the island of Lewis, based on the harbour at Stornoway. How Lowland Scotland saw the lands of the clans is unblushingly clear in the name of the company created to found a town in the Hebrides: The Gentlemen Adventurers for the Conquering of the Isles of Lewis. Most of the investors came from Fife and history remembers them as the Fife Adventurers.

In the winter of 1597–98 they sailed into Stornoway harbour and exactly in the manner of those who colonized the eastern coasts of North America they dug a ditch around their new settlement and built a stockade. And just as in Virginia and the other colonies, the indigenous inhabitants took exception. MacLeod led his clansmen in attacks on the Stornoway stockade and burned the settlement at least twice.

By 1600 the situation for the Fife Adventurers had become desperate. They had been unable to adventure far beyond their little town and their stores were running dangerously low. James Learmouth sailed out of the harbour to seek provisions. MacLeod's half-brother, Murdo, pursued him in his birlinns, boarded the Adventurers' ship and slaughtered all on board.

At that moment this extraordinary episode took an unexpected turn. MacLeod betrayed Murdo and handed him over to the king's men. Perhaps he had gone too far in killing all of the settlers' crew. Perhaps MacLeod wished to store up some future credit with the king and his privy councillors. In any event Murdo was taken to St Andrews to stand trial. Despite giving a great deal of interesting information about the ambitions of Clan Mackenzie to take over Lewis and supplant the Adventurers, he was condemned, hanged and his severed head set on a spike over the Netherbow gate into Edinburgh.

Meanwhile, in the summer of 1601, the garrison in Stornoway decided on a more aggressive approach and they boldly marched out from behind their stockade to take on the MacLeods in open country. Neil had them ambushed and at least 60 were killed. A few months later the MacLeods stormed the settlement and in return for their lives, the Adventurers agreed to quit Lewis. Neil MacLeod insisted on taking several hostages to make sure they kept their promise.

Despite their expulsion the Fife Adventurers were still seen as the legal owners of the island and they sold it to Clan Mackenzie in 1610. Under the ruthless leadership of Roderick, known as the Tutor of Kintail, the Mackenzies overran Lewis with a large force of 700 clansmen and forced Neil MacLeod to retreat to his fortress on the rocky islet of Beresay. Only when Roderick took a party of MacLeod women and children prisoners and placed them on a rock near the fortress that submerged at high tide did the defenders surrender. Two months later Neil MacLeod stood on the scaffold at Edinburgh's Mercat Cross looking desperately down the High Street for a reprieve.

The travails of the Fife Adventurers and the eventual triumph of the Mackenzies were not outcomes envisaged by James VI and his policy makers, the Privy Council, but the episode was part of a general pattern. The crown was resolved that the clans would be daunted and that the royal writ would run to every corner of the kingdom no matter how remote. And any means of achieving that aim was entirely legitimate.

In 1608 James VI (and by then James I of England and Ireland) sent an expedition to the island of Mull and its ships dropped anchor in Tobermory Bay. Nine local clan chiefs were invited on board, among other inducements, to listen to a sermon from a well-known minister. But instead of the word of God, it was a lie from the king, and the chiefs were met by armed men who immediately put them under arrest. The ships weighed anchor and the chiefs soon found themselves in prison in the Lowlands. A signature was required. If they wanted to return home, then the chiefs would have to attach their signatures and their acquiescence to a radical new piece of legislation. The Statutes

ABOVE *King James VI of Scotland and I of Great Britain and Ireland, 1610.*

of Iona were an early attempt at the eradication of a culture, the systematic dismantling of clan society.

The keepers of history, the bards, were simply banned, disabled from performing (on pain of being put in the stocks) and the sons of chiefs were compelled to be educated in the Lowlands and not fostered out and tutored by tacksmen. In 1616 an Education Act took matters a stage further, calling Gaelic *the Irish language* in one of its clauses, it was brutally clear: 'that the vulgar English tongue be planted, and the Irish language which is one of the chief and principal causes of the continuance of barbarity and incivility amongst the inhabitants of the Isles and Highlands, may be abolished and removed.'

The clans holding land on the southern edges of the Highlands were naturally the most visible to Lowland Scotland, and one in particular had the reputation of being the most troublesome. In the medieval period Clan MacGregor had occupied three glens at the head of Loch Awe: Glenstrae, Glen Orchy and Glen Lochy. Their misfortune lay to the south, for their neighbours were the powerful and expansionist Clan Campbell. Consummate politicians and aggressively acquisitive, the Campbells were anxious to take over the MacGregor glens, and they did not have to look far for an excuse. Cattle rustling was common all over the Highlands, but the MacGregors had attracted a particularly toxic reputation. And if Clan Campbell could exert some measure of control over their lawless neighbours, then the crown would look the other way.

Following the law of unintended consequences, the Campbell takeover of MacGregor territory drove the clan to live almost entirely off the proceeds of cattle raiding, thereby making the situation much worse. By 1604 James VI and I had become exasperated, but instead of sending troops or encouraging the Campbells to become even more powerful, he did something much more subtle and much more effective. He deprived the MacGregors of their name. It became a capital crime to be called MacGregor and any man who killed or robbed a member of the clan had immunity from prosecution. And that made it very dangerous to be a MacGregor.

The clan scattered, and many took other names: Drummond, Murray, Grant, even Campbell. Some would not submit. The chief, Alasdair MacGregor, and five of his tacksmen climbed the scaffold at Edinburgh's Mercat Cross and were hanged and beheaded for the crime of bearing a surname. James VI and I and his councillors had hit upon a brilliant tactic, perfectly targeted at a culture that was founded on the power of names.

MacGregors in disguise, expelled from the glens, began to make a surprising, almost immediate impact. Taking the cover-name of Gregory, several families settled in Aberdeenshire and the son of a clansman who settled at Drumoak helped the world see itself better. After graduating from the University of Aberdeen and from the University of Padua in Italy, as a member of the 'Scottish Nation', James Gregory became Professor of Mathematics at the University of St Andrews and subsequently at Edinburgh.

In 1663 Gregory published the *Optica Promota* which set down the theoretical and practical principles for constructing the world's first reflecting telescope. Much admired by Robert Hooke and Isaac Newton, Gregory also produced the first proof of the fundamental theorem of calculus. And at the simpler end of the scientific scale, he used a feather to show how sunlight split into its component colours. Gregory was a mathematical genius, without doubt, but his original insights did not occur in isolation. Many of the Gregory clan of Aberdeenshire became distinguished scholars and scientists: David Gregory invented an efficient and destructive design for a military cannon, Duncan Gregory developed algebraic theory, William Gregory was a chemist who was the first to derive morphine and codeine from opium and isoprene from rubber, and another James Gregory was Professor of Medicine at Edinburgh and he produced 'Gregory's Mixture', a famous and reliable laxative.

Descended from David Gregory's 32 children, Europe's universities saw dynasties of Gregorys occupy professorial chairs and complete many works of great scholarship. It is a surprising legacy for one of the more lawless and violent clans, but it is obscured by the reputation of the most notorious MacGregor of them all, perhaps the best-known clansman of all.

Rob Roy MacGregor was in reality an unremarkable figure, and he owes his great fame not to what he achieved but to literature. When Sir Walter Scott first heard Rob Roy's story, he quickly realized that it could be the stuff historical novels are woven around.

While his distant cousins were teaching in Scotland's universities, 'Raibeart Ruadh' or Red-haired Robert, was waiting with his clansmen to charge at the Battle of Killiecrankie in 1689. King James II had been deposed the year before and William of Orange and Mary II had been offered the throne, and Viscount Dundee had raised sympathetic Highland clans in what was the first Jacobite Rebellion. He led about 2,500 men to Blair Castle, near Pitlochry in Perthshire, for he had intelligence that a government army was marching north from Stirling. About 4,000 strong, it had some cannon and was well equipped, but if Dundee could choose the ground his Highlanders might prevail.

At the pass of Killiecrankie Glengarry narrows dramatically. Where the River Garry rushes south to join the Tummel and the Tay the track beside it is wide enough for only three men abreast or one laden pack horse. On the morning of 27 July 1689 Dundee's scouts raced back to their camp at Blair to report that General Hugh MacKay was leading his army through the pass. Needing urgently to delay MacKay and get his small army in position on the

BELOW *The death of Viscount Dundee at the Battle of Killiecrankie in 1689.*

braes above the pass, Dundee sent snipers. One man, Farquhar MacRae, managed to stop the advance of the government army, and with two firelock muskets and a comrade to reload them, he kept the advancing soldiers' heads down long enough.

Meanwhile Dundee quickly led his Highlanders up to a commanding ridge just to the north of the pass. Once MacRae had fallen back and the government soldiers were finally through Killiecrankie their advance guard reported the enemy position and General MacKay (himself a clansman loyal to William of Orange) gave the order for his troops to follow them up to the higher ground. Beyond some woodland stood the Jacobite army, looking down from a crest.

It was late afternoon and very warm and sunny. Dundee instructed his captains to tell their men to do nothing, hold their positions, sit on their shields and wait for further orders. It was something of an anti-climax and the Camerons especially were itching to fight. MacKay's artillery began firing, attempting to goad the clans into action. They sat still. Dundee was waiting for the westering sun to move around behind his army, and blind the government soldiers who were forced to look up the slope. At around 7 pm the pipers blew, the clansmen stood to, those who had muskets fired a volley and all raised their broadswords. Screaming their war cries, they raced into the downhill charge, running at a tremendous pace. Rob Roy MacGregor charged with them. Only 18 years old, it was his first adrenalin taste of war.

MacKay's troops fired a returning volley, but the clans came on so fast that few had time to fix bayonets. In the late 17th century they were rammed into the barrel of a musket and when the first wave of Highlanders smashed into the government lines they were swept away. As men ran for their lives, stumbling and panicking, the narrow pass of Killiecrankie choked and became a killing ground. But the Jacobites also took severe casualties, especially under musket fire, and one of these was Viscount Dundee, John Graham of Claverhouse. A brilliant and ruthless commander (known as 'Bluidy Clavers'), he had been the central figure of the 1689 rebellion and with his death it fizzled out.

Rob Roy and his fellow clansmen saw the ban on their name renewed in 1694, and Rob Roy took the alternative of Campbell. After buying land at

OPPOSITE *An 18th-century representation of what Rob Roy MacGregor is thought to have looked like.*

Craigroyston and Inversnaid, east of Loch Lomond, Rob Roy began to prosper, dealing in and rearing cattle. Renting good grazing on the south-facing braes at Balquhidder in Perthshire, he fattened herds before driving them to the markets at the Falkirk Trysts. But in 1711 his business collapsed

ABOVE *John Graham of Claverhouse, Viscount Dundee (1648–89).*

OVERLEAF *The Battle of Glen Shiel, a rare Jacobite defeat in the Highlands, fought in 1719.*

and Rob Roy was gazetted as an outlaw. He had borrowed £1,000 to buy more stock, but his chief drover, a MacDonald, made off with the cash and he was left with debts he could not repay. Evicted from his house at Craigroyston, he was hunted through the glens by government soldiers and forced to become a cattle rustler.

When the clans rose once more in rebellion in 1715 and in 1719, Rob Roy marched with them, and was badly wounded in the defeat at the Battle of Glen Shiel. But taking advantage of an amnesty in 1725, he submitted to the English commander, General Wade, and nine years later Rob Roy MacGregor died in his bed aged 63.

It sounds a simple enough story, but all was not quite as it seems. Far from being merely a rebellious outlaw and cattle thief, Rob Roy probably went to university, matriculating at Glasgow between 1683 and 1685. His elder brother was recorded as an undergraduate before him. Not only could he read and write fluently in both English and Gaelic (some of his letters have survived), but enjoying books, and history in particular, Rob Roy was listed as a subscriber to a limited edition of Bishop Keith's *History of the Scottish Reformation*. And it was literature that would make him famous.

Sir Walter Scott was a phenomenon, the inventor of the bestseller, and in his own right, one of the most famous Scots in the world. He may have named his novel *Rob Roy*, but it is really the story of an Englishman, Francis Osbaldistone, set in the time of Jacobite Rebellion of 1715. The story also features one of Scott's most colourful characters in Bailie Nicol Jarvie. Because the fame and reach of Scott's work was worldwide and unprecedented, Rob Roy MacGregor and the Highland clans also emerged onto a world stage, at least in a fictional version.

Much of the modern perception of Highlanders and Highland culture dates from 1818, the year of the novel's publication, but that is to anticipate events – and by some distance.

6

No Further than Here

 ITHOUT DOUBT THE CAMPBELLS WERE THE MOST CONSISTENTLY SUCCESSFUL OF ALL THE HIGHLAND CLANS. Led by a series of capable and courageous chiefs, they expanded their territory in the south-west and in Perthshire, and by the 18th century had become almost irresistible. Clan Campbell could muster what amounted to an army and were capable of sending 5,000 men into battle in defence and pursuit of its interests.

Now Dukes of Argyll, Campbell chiefs also all take a much more ancient and hard-won title. MacCailean Mor, the Son of Great Colin, remembers the warrior who established the name. By the end of the 13th century Sir Colin Campbell had acquired land around Loch Awe and his elder brother held Strachur on Loch Fyne. These properties formed the core of the vast estates that eventually came under the control of the Campbells.

Like the MacDonalds, the clan profited by their loyalty to Robert the Bruce, and they rarely lost influence at the royal court after that time. Geography helped. Campbell country was closer to central Scotland, and in their birlinns the chiefs could move around easily and quickly, sailing up the long sea-lochs which reached into the heart of their territory. By 1457 they had become Earls of Argyll and, after the fall of the MacDonald Lordship of the Isles, became masters of the most powerful clan in the Highlands.

The Campbells became the king's enforcers and when disorder or rebellion broke out they usually took the side of central authority. After the Reformation of the 1560s, the chiefs were staunch Protestants (although it is likely that many clansmen remained Catholic for much longer) and when the National Covenant was drawn up in 1638, the Earl of Argyll, Archibald Campbell, signed it. The Covenant was a peculiarly Scottish political movement that vigorously opposed Charles I's attempts to introduce the Anglican prayer book (in effect merging the Church of Scotland and the Church of England), and it quickly flared into violence.

One of the four young noblemen involved in framing the National Covenant was James Graham, Marquis of Montrose. With great patriotic passion, he and the others believed that God had a direct and unique covenant with the people of Scotland, what the reformers had called 'Christ's Kingdom of Scotland'. No priests with their mumbo-jumbo or bishops in their finery were needed to intercede because through the priesthood of all believers each man and woman was personally responsible for the salvation of their immortal souls, and had an immediate relationship with God. Since the upheavals of the 1560s Scotland has striven to become a literate nation, so that all of its people would be able to read the Bible, the Word of God, for themselves without the need for interpretation. And astonishingly the National Covenant ultimately attracted more than 300,000 signatures, almost a third of the population.

In the early years of the war between Charles I and those who, for different reasons, opposed him in England, Scotland and Ireland, Montrose fought with the armies of the Covenant. The Campbell chiefs were also committed Covenanters, but when matters intensified and the Scottish Parliament drew up the Solemn League and Covenant in 1643 (this promised Scottish help in the war with the king on condition that England's parliament agreed that the nation would convert to a Scottish form of Presbyterianism), Montrose began to waver. Having been imprisoned in Edinburgh Castle for five months, he changed sides and began a brilliant year-long campaign in support of the royalist cause. And in so doing, he would involve the Highland clans in national politics.

Montrose was a gifted soldier. Charismatic, tactically astute and possessed of great physical courage, he could inspire his men to amazing victories against all odds. In 1644 he was joined by another immensely talented general: known as Alasdair MacColla, but in reality a MacDonald, he led a force of Irish warriors and men from those clans who opposed the Campbells. This was to be a recurring theme throughout the next century. The national issues of the kingdom and its king were often secondary to the more local – and much sharper – antagonism between the Campbells and many of the other Highland clans. And MacColla himself appears to have had old scores to settle.

Montrose and the MacDonald general met at Blair Atholl. They immediately resolved to march on Perth and at Tippermuir, four miles west of the city, they met a larger and better equipped force of Covenanters under the command of Lord Elcho. It was the first time the ferocious Celtic charge was seen in modern times, but it was led by Irishmen as well as Highlanders. Few were killed in the engagement itself, but when the charge put the Covenanter troops to flight more than 2,000 were cut down as they ran. Perth had been taken for the crown and the first in a dramatic sequence of victories had been won.

It was September 1644 and immediately after the battle MacColla rode west to raise more of the MacDonalds and the clans who opposed the Campbells. Two months later Montrose welcomed companies of men from Clan Ranald, Glengarry, Keppoch, Sleat and Glencoe. The Stewarts of Appin had also come with MacColla to fight for Charles I and there were Camerons and other, smaller groups. An impressive army had at last mustered.

Montrose's strategy was to descend with fire and sword on the Lowlands and thereby draw Scottish regiments away from the civil war in England. Cromwell and the other Parliamentarian commanders had come to depend heavily on the battle-hard Scottish veterans, many of whom had fought in the Thirty Years War in Europe. But MacColla would have none of it. His men would go no further south, but instead he insisted on moving south-west through the Highland passes to the country of the Campbells and their castle at Inveraray. Montrose had no choice.

ABOVE *James Graham, Marquis of Montrose, painted by Willem van Honthorst.*

It was December 1644 and there was deep snow. Bitter winter winds whipped across the mountains. No army could advance and far less campaign in such weather. Archibald Campbell sat snug by his roaring fire in Inveraray Castle, secure in the certainty that nothing would happen until the following spring.

On 13 December shepherds at the head of Glen Shira saw a remarkable thing. Over the snow-covered plateau by Loch Stron Mor an army was marching towards them. There were thousands: MacDonalds, Stewarts, Irish warriors and on shaggy garron ponies rode Montrose, MacColla and all their captains. Loch Fyne lay at the foot of Glen Shira and the town of Inveraray and the Campbell castle were less than a mile further south. When he heard the unbelievable news that an army was an hour from his walls, Earl Archibald had no choice but to flee. There was no time to raise a defence, scarcely enough time to get his family to safety. Once his oarsmen had pulled their chief's birlinn out into the loch he will have watched the MacDonalds and Montrose's army march along the shore road. Perhaps their insults and taunts carried across the water. Campbell knew what would happen next.

The town and the farms around were destroyed by MacColla's men and he became feared in Argyll as 'fear thollaidh nan tighean', the breaker of houses. There was an appalling massacre. Any Campbell clansman old enough to fight was killed outright and it is thought that 900 men died, some very cruelly. The contemporary Covenanter historian, Robert Baillie, expressed a general amazement at the audacity of MacColla and the hardihood of his men:

> The world believed that Argyll could be maintained against the greatest army, as a country inaccessible, but we see there is no strength or refuge on earth against the Lord.

Laden with plunder, the royalist army climbed back over the mountains and made their way to Appin and Stewart country to rest and regroup. On 8 January Montrose led his men up the Great Glen, but at the foot of Loch Ness he was met by Iain Lom, the famous MacDonald bard of Keppoch. His news was not good. Two Covenanter armies were closing in, one at either end of the glen. Montrose and MacColla would have to cut their way out of a trap.

At Inverness the Earl of Seaforth, chief of Clan Mackenzie, had mustered troops, while at Inverlochy Castle, near Fort William, 2,000 Campbells and 1,000 Lowlanders waited under the command of an experienced and tough soldier, Sir Duncan Campbell of Auchinbreck. Seaforth was known to be an unenthusiastic Covenanter and his force was the smaller. But Montrose and MacColla decided to turn south and attack the much stronger Campbells. Their reasoning was simple. There was hatred involved. With an army of MacDonalds, Stewarts and MacDonnells there was no need to incite them to fight. Their blood enemies were waiting at Inverlochy.

Sir Duncan remembered the Field of the Shirts, when John of Moidart had destroyed the Frasers between Loch Lochy and Loch Oich, and he was determined to fight on open ground where his superior numbers could be decisive. The army camped at Inverlochy, near the castle, where the Great Glen widens. Campbell scouts searched the north road by the banks of Loch Lochy for Montrose's men. They had to come that way, there was no other route, no other possible choice.

Even with the MacDonald reinforcements, Montrose and MacColla's force was smaller, perhaps only half the Campbell strength. If they were to be caught in an open field they could quickly be outflanked, find an enemy behind them and be slaughtered. Perhaps a march on Inverness and a wavering Seaforth was more sensible after all.

Montrose was a graduate of the University of St Andrews, and it may be that at that decisive moment he remembered his ancient history. Hannibal, the great Carthaginian general, had led his army – and its war elephants – through the Alpine passes and on to victory after victory over the Romans. The Highlanders and the tough Irish regiments had shown tremendous endurance in the descent on Inveraray only a month before. That audacious stroke had brought victory, and plunder. Perhaps there was a way to avoid meeting the Campbells on ground of their choosing at Inverlochy.

The Camerons knew of a high pass to the south of the Great Glen. It threaded between two mountains, Carn Dearg and Carn Leac, but it was only possible in good weather and in the summer. But in the deep snows of January and its numbing cold, the pass of the *Allt na Larach*, the Scar Burn, could not be crossed. It climbed to more than 2,000 feet, men could be lost in its snowdrifts or die of cold and exhaustion, their legs drained, their plaids frozen. The Cameron scouts shook their heads.

But their captains were not listening. Somehow Montrose and MacColla persuaded their men to make their way into the winter mountains. First they struck south off the Great Glen and into Glen Tarff, which opens at the foot of Loch Ness. Following the icy, fast-flowing stream, they quickly climbed through the snow-line and using sticks to probe the drifts, men took turns in the vanguard to find a path. Carn Dearg loomed high above, but it screened the long lines of clansmen from the Great Glen. No Campbell scout would ever have ventured as far as the *Allt na Larach*. When darkness fell and temperatures plummeted, the Highlanders kept moving through the long January night. The snow reflected what little moonlight there was.

ABOVE *The ruins of Inverlochy Castle. It was through the mountains behind that Montrose's men marched in the snow in 1645.*

Towards dawn the men at the head of the column could see that the ground was at last beginning to fall away and that at the head of Glen Roy there was a track. Probably led by Camerons, whose country this was, the army quickly made their way down off the mountains and along the road by the River Spean. Their heroic, epic march had taken 36 hours, but the Campbells watching the Great Glen road had no idea that Montrose had circled round and was about to appear on their flank.

The plan almost misfired. Parts of Montrose's army made contact with the Campbells and skirmishing broke out. But Sir Duncan judged that it was no more than a raiding party, perhaps a band of Camerons intent on minor mischief. How could it be anything else? Throughout that day Montrose and MacColla kept their main force concealed, but ready to stand to at a moment's notice.

When dawn broke on 2 February 1645 the Campbell captains were thunderstruck at the sight of the whole royalist army drawn up in battle order, ready to attack their flank. Montrose disposed his forces brilliantly. Knowing that his charge would scatter the Lowlanders in Sir Duncan's army, he set MacColla and his Irish regiments opposite them. Under his own command in the centre stood most of the Highland clansmen. They would deal with the Campbell contingents, men like themselves, used to fighting hand to hand with sword and dirk.

ABOVE *Archibald Campbell, Earl of Argyll, and his wife, c.1660s.*

When the claidheamh mor sounded MacColla's men fired a single volley and tore into the Lowlanders. Despite their ranks being stiffened with detachments of Campbells, they broke and ran. In the centre a ferocious fight raged between the MacDonalds and the Campbells. Few hacked and stabbed for king, parliament or even the reformed religion. At Inverlochy one of the most vicious clan battles in history took place.

Exposed on their flanks to MacColla and his Irishmen, the Campbells began to give ground. And then in a moment, it seemed, their resistance crumbled. Men retreated into the lines behind them, they panicked, and the momentum was with Montrose and the MacDonalds. Once again more men died in the flight than in the fighting. Some drowned in Loch Linnhe, desperately attempting to flee from MacDonald fury. Perhaps 1,500 died. Sir Duncan fell and those who tried to find refuge in Inverlochy Castle were cut down before they could reach it.

It was the heaviest, most disastrous defeat ever suffered by a Campbell army, and Iain Lom was exultant, his poem gloating over the victory gained by his clan, nowhere mentioning the king or the royalist cause:

Early on Sunday morning I climbed the brae above
the castle of Inverlochy.
I saw the army arrayed for battle,
And victory in the field was with Clan Donald...

You remember the place called the Tawny Field.
It was manured, not with the dung of sheep or goats,
But by the blood of Campbells, well congealed.
To Hell with you if I feel pity for your plight,
As I listen to the distress of your children,
Lamenting the band that went into battle,
The wailing of the women of Argyll.

The anger is palpable – on both sides. Sir Duncan's sister wrote:

Were I at Inverlochy, with a two-edged sword in my hand,
And all the strength and skill I could desire,
I would draw blood there,
And I would tear asunder the MacLeans and the MacDonalds.
The Irish would be without life.
And I would bring the Campbells back to life.

Inverlochy broke the power of the Campbells for a generation. At Inverness Seaforth declared for Charles I and other clans joined the royalist cause. Montrose and MacColla won more victories, and by the late summer of 1645 the army was at last in the Lowlands. But when they came to Philiphaugh, near Selkirk, MacColla and his clansmen had gone. After a year of stunning success the two great commanders were never to meet again. Without his fearsome Highlanders, Montrose was heavily defeated by a Covenanter army that marched north from the civil war in England.

The restoration of Charles II in 1660 brought to an end a long period of war and instability in the Highlands. Despite their defeats by Montrose and MacColla, the Campbells recovered and emerged once more as the overwhelming political force in the north and west. Archibald Campbell, the 9th Earl of Argyll, now operated as the king's lieutenant, but it was through their economic dominance that the clan began to press hard on their neighbours.

By the 1670s the chiefs of the MacLeans owed the Campbells a vast sum, in excess of 200,000 merks, and Clan Ranald was also deep in debt to them. Land was perfectly acceptable as payment in lieu and with the use of force, both threatened and actual, as well as the law, Clan Campbell expanded. Not without a hard fight, the MacLeans lost much of Mull and their stronghold at Duart Castle, while the islands of Islay and Tiree fell under Campbell control.

Enmities between clans festered like sores, were rarely resolved and often the motivation for what can seem like random violence in the Highlands. And few clans loathed each other with such passion as did the Campbells and the Mac-Donalds. One of the most notorious atrocities in Scottish history was perpetrated by one of these clans on the other, but despite appearances it sprang directly from the calculations of national politics and was part of no ancient feud.

After the replacement of James VII with William of Orange and Mary II in 1688, London and Edinburgh worried about the allegiances of the western clans – all except the Campbells. It was decided that the chiefs should swear an oath of loyalty and a deadline was set for 1 January 1692. Many of the chiefs contacted the exiled James VII for permission to make the submission and after much dithering, it was granted by mid-December. That left little time for the formalities to be observed. MacIan, chief of the MacDonalds of Glencoe, was late, but not for the want of trying.

It was a deep and snowy winter as the old chief set out for the government garrison at Inverlochy Castle. Mistakenly believing that his old friend, Colonel Hill, could administer the oath, MacIan was horrified to discover that he had in fact to make his way to Inveraray, a very long way to the south. Nevertheless, fully realizing the importance of this loyalty test, he reached the town a few days later – only to find that the Sheriff was absent on holiday after the New Year celebrations. MacIan waited. And several days later he signed his name as a loyal subject of William of Orange. It was not to be enough to save him and his people.

John Dalrymple, the Master of Stair, and Secretary of State for Scotland, saw the breaking of the deadline as an opportunity to make an example. 'It could be a proper vindication of public justice to extirpate that sept of thieves.' These were not the words of Dalrymple or a vengeful henchman, but part of a statement signed WR, or William Rex, King William I. The Highland clans would be taught a lesson. The Glencoe MacDonalds were to be massacred, all of them, and approval for this appalling proposal had, literally, the seal of royal approval. As MacIan made his way back through the winter from Inveraray plans were laid.

ABOVE *James VII and II, the last Stuart king to reign in London. This portrait was painted by Sir Peter Lely.*

ABOVE Massacre of Glencoe *by James Hamilton (1883–86). A band of MacDonalds are in hiding from the Campbell soldiers down in Glencoe.*

On 1 February Robert Campbell of Glenlyon led a company of soldiers who happened to be Campbell clansmen, but were nevertheless soldiers in the British army acting under specific orders, into Glencoe. Since the MacDonalds had yet to pay their taxes, troops could be billeted in their houses. Glenlyon had their orders in writing: 'You are hereby ordered to fall upon the rebels, the MacDonalds of Glencoe and put all to the sword under seventy.' The soldiers waited five days, becoming familiar, even friendly with their hosts. Once both ends of Glencoe had been sealed by companies of soldiers, so that there could be no escape, the killing began. At dawn on 6 February soldiers cut the throats of MacIan, his wife and two of their younger sons. Another 34 MacDonalds were slaughtered and many who ran for their lives later died of exposure in the snow. There is some evidence that the Campbell soldiers allowed many to flee.

It would not have happened in the Lowlands. The Massacre of Glencoe was meted out to people who were considered savages, sub-humans who spoke a barbarous language and lived in primitive conditions in a wild and uncivilized landscape. Sadly it was an extreme, even shocking, example of the widening gulf between clan society and the rest of Scotland. But even by the standards of the time it was thought a disgrace, a shameful episode and a stain on history.

7

MOMENTS WHEN NOTHING SEEMED IMPOSSIBLE

OLL MACDONALD, THE CHIEF OF THE MACDONALDS OF KEPPOCH, had enjoyed the University of St Andrews, but he never managed to graduate. In 1682 his father died and the young student found himself back in Lochaber dealing with an angry man. The Clan Chattan Confederation held ancient title to lands in Lochaber which had long been appropriated by MacDonald squatters and Lachlan Mackintosh, their chief, was demanding that their property be returned forthwith. As an educated man, Coll sought to settle the matter peacefully and came to Inverness with some of his tacksmen whereupon hands were laid on him and the Chief of Keppoch suffered the indignity of being thrown into prison like a common criminal. Although he was quickly released, Coll never forgot the offence.

In 1688 Mackintosh was granted a commission of fire and sword, that is, the right to remove the MacDonalds by force. A detachment of government troops was put at his disposal and with their commander, Captain Kenneth Mackenzie, the Chief of Clan Chattan marched unopposed into Lochaber in late July. Coll was waiting.

Having summoned his kinsmen from Glengarry and Glencoe, and been joined by the MacMartins, a sept of Clan Cameron, the Chief of Keppoch chose his ground. With 800 clansmen, the MacDonalds took up a position on Maol Ruadh, a prominent hill overlooking the mouth of their glen. Believing that with a force twice as large they would certainly prevail, Mackintosh and Mackenzie made the cardinal error of advancing uphill against Highlanders. One of the government soldiers was Donald MacBane, a former tobacco spinner from Inverness, and he left a remarkable record of what happened next. Vivid, honest and sardonic, it is a rare memoir of what it was like to face a Highland charge:

The two clans were both on foot and our company was still with Mackintosh, who marched towards MacDonald and his clan, until we came in sight of them (which made me wish I had been spinning tobacco). Mackintosh sent one of his friends to MacDonald to treat with him, and see if he would come to reasonable terms. MacDonald directly denied, but would fight it by the event as it would [turn out]. Then both parties ordered their men to march up the hill, a company being in the front, we drew up in line of battle as we could, our company being on the right. We were no sooner in order but there appears double our number of the MacDonalds, which made us then fear the worst, at least for my part. I repeated my former wish (I never having seen the like). The MacDonalds came down the hill upon us without either shoe, stocking or bonnet on their head. They gave a shout and then the fire began on both sides, and continued a hot dispute for an hour. Then they broke in upon us with sword and targe, and Lochaber axes, which obliged us to give way. Seeing my captain sore wounded, and a great many more with heads lying cloven on every side, I was sadly affrighted, never having seen the like before. A Highlander attacked me with sword and targe and cut my wooden-handled bayonet out of the muzzle of my gun. I then clubbed my gun and gave him a stroke with it, which made the butt-end fly off. Seeing the Highland men

come fast upon me, I took to my heels and ran thirty miles before I looked behind me. Every person I saw or met, I took for my enemy.

It was the last clan battle and despite the fleeting presence of government soldiers, it was the last time two clans faced each to fight a pitched battle to settle an issue between them. And the victorious Coll MacDonald was soon able to put his experience to more famous use. A year later he was at Killiecrankie with Viscount Dundee, and almost certainly had a telling influence on strategy. After the clans charged out of the sun and put General Hugh MacKay's troops to flight, one man gained immortality by jumping 18 feet across the River Garry to escape to safety. Visitors are now directed to the site of 'The Soldier's Leap' and told that it was made by none other than Donald MacBane.

Despite the death of Dundee at Killiecrankie, the Highland army pressed on southwards. Realizing that their objective was likely to be the cathedral town of Dunkeld, the Scottish Privy Council ordered the regiment of the Cameronians to occupy and defend it. And the Battle of Dunkeld would turn on the name of Cameron and the competing passions of two men who bore it.

OPPOSITE AND BELOW *Members of the regiment of the 43rd Highlanders. Foot soldiers wore kilts while cavalry sported tartan trews.*

After the loss of their commander, the Jacobite army was led down Strathtay by Colonel Alexander Cannon, one of the senior Irish soldiers to join the rebellion. Old Sir Ewan Cameron of Locheil, greatly respected and the most formidable of the clan chiefs to march under Dundee's banner, was mortified and so insulted not to be asked to assume command that he chose to return to Lochaber with most of his clansmen.

The Cameronian regiment that was busy fortifying Dunkeld shared only a name with Sir Ewan. These soldiers had been recruited mainly in Lanarkshire by the charismatic Covenanter preacher, Richard Cameron, and they became quickly known for their courage and stubbornness. When Lt Colonel Cleland and his men arrived in Dunkeld they realized that its defence would have to concentrate around the cathedral. There was no town wall, only a high dyke around the cathedral precinct, intended to mark off the sacred area and not defend it. Those townspeople who barricaded themselves in their houses beyond the precinct would regret rejecting Cleland's strong advice to leave.

On 21 August 1689 lookouts in the cathedral tower raised the alarm: they could see the Highland army approaching from the north. The streets emptied and the Cameronians took up their positions on the wall, readied themselves and primed their muskets for the onslaught. Outnumbering the defenders by four to one, even with the departure of Clan Cameron, the Jacobites wasted no time and charged. But the wall held, and again and again the clansmen came on, and again and again they were thrown back. The narrow streets and lanes were entirely unsuited to Highland tactics and men armed mainly with bladed weapons. The volleys of the Cameronian muskets kept them back and unable to engage in hand-to-hand fighting in their mounting frustration the clansmen fired at several barricaded houses and those cowering inside suffered horrific deaths.

When Cleland was fatally wounded, struck by musket balls in his chest and head, he died a heroic death. So that his men might not witness it and become disheartened at the loss of their captain, Cleland summoned the last shreds of his strength and dragged himself out of sight. The battle raged around the old cathedral for 16 hours until finally the Highlanders withdrew at around 11 pm. Three hundred of them lay dead in the streets, and the exhausted defenders had also taken grievous casualties. But they had held the

OPPOSITE *Sir Ewan Cameron of Locheil (1629–1719) in his prime.*

town. While Ewan Cameron sulked in the Lochaber glens, the first Jacobite rebellion was broken against the stones of a Scottish cathedral and men inspired by another Cameron. Less than a year later, at the Haughs of Cromdale on Speyside, a remnant of the Highland army was routed and dispersed by government cavalry. In May 1690 General MacKay had his men build Fort William, named for the new king, near Inverlochy Castle. In Gaelic, the alternative place name is blunt, making no mention of William of Orange: *An Gearasdan* simply means the garrison. Eventually it would become the southern end of a line of three government garrisons: Fort Augustus in the Great Glen and Fort George on the Moray Firth near Inverness. In July 1690 James VII and II was defeated at the Battle of the Boyne in Ireland and the Jacobite cause took a generation to regroup.

The author of *Robinson Crusoe* made a great mistake when he looked out of the window of his lodgings at Moubray House in Edinburgh's High Street. There was a great commotion below and when the mob recognized Daniel Defoe they pelted him with stones and rubbish. His crime was to have been an Englishman in Scotland's capital city in 1707. A few yards up the High Street, next to the High Kirk of St Giles, the Scottish Parliament was in the process of voting itself out of existence. The proposed Act of Union was deeply unpopular, as Defoe reported to his masters in London, and the Edinburgh mob was incensed, rioting violently when it was finally passed. Perhaps they would have done more than pelt him with stones if the rioters had known that the novelist was an English spy.

'Bought and sold for English gold' lamented a Jacobite song and it was true. Bribes, open and covert, had eased the passage of the bill and another English spy sent a despatch saying that most Scots hated the noblemen who so shamelessly sold their nation, and that for every one man for the Union, there were fifty against it. 'I never saw a nation so universally wild', he wrote.

For the Jacobite cause, the Act of Union was a political gift. James VII and II had died in 1701 and been succeeded by his son, also James. With the support of France, Europe's greatest military power, the Jacobites seemed set to act decisively, at least in Scotland. In 1708, less than a year after the unpopular act came into effect, James VIII and III sailed from Dunkirk with a fleet of 30 French ships and 4,500 soldiers aboard. They aimed to make landfall in Scotland, on the shores of the Firth of Forth. Substantial support was waiting and under the leadership of John Murray, Duke of Atholl, both clansmen and lowland sympathizers planned to rally to the Stuart standard. Probably the best chance for Jacobite success, the expedition of 1708 was defeated by bad luck, bad weather, poor communications and worse seamanship. With a squadron of Royal Navy men of war, Admiral Byng confronted the French fleet, panicked its captains and chased them up the North Sea coast and around the farthest shores of Scotland. Like the Spanish Armada in 1588, some ships were dashed to pieces on the jagged Atlantic coast, and James VIII and III's hopes were dashed along with them.

The world of the clans was changing and by the outset of the 18th century many of the chiefs had sensed it. In the hundred or so years since the Statutes of Iona and the move of the royal court to London *oigreachd* had come to dominate and the notion that clan lands belonged personally to the chief and his family could be seen in the decline of tanistry and fosterage. The Dukes of Argyll and others became great magnates, significant figures of influence at the London court. *Dùthchas* was fading into the darkness of the past. Clansmen and their families may still have felt an umbilical attachment to their ancient territory but in no meaningful sense was it any longer theirs. In the 18th and 19th centuries war and grim economics would sweep away all the traditions of customary right no matter that countless generations had walked their lives in the same glens and under the same huge Highland skies.

Nevertheless chiefs still exerted absolute power over their clan. When their people refused to abandon old townships on Skye, two chiefs took summary action. Both MacLeod of Dunvegan and MacDonald of Sleat evicted large groups and deported them by forcing them onto transport ships bound for North America. And a Clan Ranald chief was still cruelly executing those found guilty of what seem now to have been trivial offences. On one notorious occasion a thief suffered a terrible death by being bound hand and foot and having her hair tied to the wrack and seaweed below the high tideline.

External pressures were also brought to bear. Gaelic was routinely described as Irish in order to make the language appear foreign, not British. And at the beginning of the 18th century concerted efforts were underway to discourage Gaelic and eventually destroy it. Founded in 1708, the Society for the Propagating of Christian Knowledge (SPCK) was in the vanguard, insisting on the use of an English Bible and making bluntly obvious links between language, religion and politics. Here is a telling fragment from a SPCK report:

Many of those Highlanders, etc., are in an interest absolutely inconsistent with the safety of the Government, for they are bred in principles of tyranny, depend upon the Pope as Head of the Church, upon a Popish Pretender bred up in the arbitrary maxims of France as their rightful sovereign.

It was not true. Very few of the clans were Catholic, most followed their chief's lead and the majority were Episcopalians. But the government and its doctrinal agents mounted an assault, the effects of which are still felt, on the Gaelic language. English was portrayed as the language of the future and Gaelic spoke only of the past. The same corrosive process was underway in Ireland where the influential author of *Gulliver's Travels* was railing and pamphleteering against Irish Gaelic. Jonathan Swift was characteristically vicious in his dismissal of the barbarisms uttered by native Irish speakers. It did nothing but drag them down into the mire of poverty and incivility. Only recently have attitudes altered.

The language of the clans and their culture was particularly vulnerable because so little of it had been written down. As the numbers of speakers declined (in 1769, the very earliest date for any sort of record, it is thought that 23 per cent, or 290,000, of Scotland's population of 1,265,000 spoke Gaelic. Now it is only 50,000 out of a population in excess of 5,000,000, or less than one per cent) the richness of the language and its dialects died with them.

Gaelic is a language of memory, structured and refined for ease of recall, not a literary medium as English has become. Celtic society retained its sense of itself, its history, its customs, its laws and all its lore in the memories of specialists, the bards or seannachies. Remnants remain, but not in Scotland. At the ancient parliament of the Isle of Man, the *Tynwald*, lawyers known as deemsters read out any new Manx laws to the assembled crowds, and it is not until they have been read out – in Manx Gaelic – that they become law. These can be mundane; building regulations or measures to keep Manx law in line with British legislation, but when they are read by the deemsters the law is known as *breast law*, an allusion to codification by memory.

Modern romantics beguiled by the mist and the mountains sometimes talk of the poetry of Gaelic and convey an impression of a windy vagueness, but in fact the language is as lexically tight and precise as Ciceronian Latin. Gaelic has a range and complexity, especially when it deals with

the natural world, now lost in English. Colour offers good examples. Few now understand that the old English word *brindled* means 'streaked with irregular dark shades', but Gaels still use *riabhach* to mean the same thing. In the spectrum vaguely described as beige, parchment or the colour of porridge, Gaelic has subtleties like *lachdann* and *odhar* to pin down the precise pigment. The adjectives were all used to describe the colour of cattle and in any dispute the ability to describe accurately whose cows were whose could be vital.

There is no word for yes or for no in Gaelic. It is difficult to imagine how a language might function without such basic equipment, but the effect is to make Gaelic much more precise. When a question is asked, the reply must use the verb in either the affirmative or the negative. 'Are you hungry?' requires either 'I am' or 'I am not'. No ambiguity is possible.

Cases have also survived. There are genitives and datives, but perhaps the most striking is the persistent use of the vocative case. When someone is addressed directly the first syllable of their name is altered, usually by adding an 'h' in a process known as aspiration. Two of the most common have passed into use as Scottish christian names and few who baptise their children as Mhairi (pronounced Vari) realize that it is the Gaelic vocative of Mairi or Mary, or that Hamish is the vocative of Seamas or James.

Many words associated with weather also have no direct translation or need a phrase as an equivalent. *Tioradh* means a dry interval between bands of rain coming in off the ocean. *Sluaisreadh* (pronounced slewashrugh) is a beautiful onomatopoeia for the action of the indrawn tide washing over the shoreline. Precision and grace – and great beauty. Spoken by a fluent Gael, the language is very beautiful, even to an uncomprehending ear. It is sometimes called the language of Eden.

Clan society understood itself in Gaelic and when the language began to decline it was inevitable that the Highlands would change and lose much of its identity. A peculiarly poignant example of that cultural loss can be seen on a map. Highland geography is almost all named in Gaelic and even those who walk and love the mountains and the high passes have difficulty in pronouncing their right names.

The Act of Union did confer one significant benefit. It opened up hungry English markets to Highland cattle, not the shaggy, long-horned creatures of the biscuit tin lid, but the small black cattle that grazed the glens. As the towns of England began to industrialize into cities, the demand for beef grew and the drovers became important to the Highland economy. Many were clansmen, like Rob Roy MacGregor, and they made their way into the glens and across to the islands to buy herds from producers. Cattle had to be shipped from the Outer Hebrides, but from Skye the beasts swam across the Atlantic, across the narrow straits at Kylerhea. It must have been an extraordinary sight.

The cattle trade changed what had been a subsistence economy into one which might produce profits. As the 18th century wore on chiefs will have noted that the Highland landscape could rear animals that were much more immediately valuable than the low rents paid by their tenants, no matter how long their forebears had worked the rigs and tended the shielings. It was a baleful harbinger of things to come.

Language and religion mattered to the SPCK and they were seen as intimately connected to sedition. The London government feared the clans and the alarming speed with which the chiefs could muster an army. The Campbell Earl of Breadalbane did some arithmetic for a report to William of Orange. More than 30,000 clansmen could quickly muster under the Stuart banner, he reckoned, and because of their unquestioning devotion to the chiefs they were very dangerous – and more reliable than the recruits of a standing army. Breadalbane recommended that the British army should encourage the raising of Highland regiments and thereby remove warlike elements to follow the service of the king. Sixty years later, Breadalbane's good advice would be taken.

Meanwhile the wheels of dynastic change turned once more. Queen Anne, who had at least been a Stuart of some sort, died childless in 1714 and was succeeded by a German aristocrat, George, the Elector of Hanover. It was the signal for another Stuart attempt on the throne.

The initial impetus came from rejection and a monumental sulk. John Erskine, 6th Earl of Mar, had been Queen Anne's Secretary of State for Scotland and when George I (also known as George of Hanover) arrived in London, he made the great mistake of making assumptions. In a sycophantic letter of welcome, Erskine promised the new king his continuing loyalty as the royal representative in Scotland. Unimpressed, George I asked the earl for his seals of office and summarily dismissed him. Furious, Mar immediately took ship, any ship – apparently he sailed on a collier bound for Newcastle – and when he finally disembarked at Aberdeen and made his way to his estates on Deeside, he had become a Jacobite.

Known as 'Bobbing John', Mar was well connected and powerful, but his motives for raising the Stuart standard in 1715 were to taint the rebellion from the outset. Under the thin pretence of a grand hunting party, he summoned clan chiefs and northern noblemen to meet him at Braemar in August. By 6 September he was proclaiming James VIII and III as the lawful sovereign, and both the clans and supporters of lowland magnates rallied to the cause. At least they were passionate. Longstanding grievances were buried as Mackintoshes joined MacDonalds of Keppoch and MacDonalds of Glencoe marched alongside Glenlyon Campbells under the royal banners. But there was also evidence of reluctance. Tacksmen had always had to make threats to turn out all their clansmen, but Mar warned those of his tenants unwilling to fight that his men would burn them out.

Despite this and the lack of emphatic leadership, the 1715 rebellion could have been successful. It was not a purely Highland affair: support came not only from lowland Scotland, but also northern England. And risings had been plotted in Wales, Devon and Cornwall – although, in the event they were forestalled when government agents arrested local Jacobites.

On 14 September Mar's army took Perth unopposed. There were 8,000 at his back and in Scotland opposition was ill-prepared. The Duke of Argyll held Stirling, but had only 2,000 men. For once momentum and numbers were running strongly in the Jacobites' favour. Mar sent William Mackintosh south with 2,000 men to link up with contingents raised in the Borders and Northumberland. They marched into England, past Carlisle, across

BELOW *The Battle of Sheriffmuir, 1715.*

the Westmorland fells and down into Lancashire. But the hoped-for recruits did not flock to the cause and by Sunday 12 November the Highlanders and their lowland allies found themselves besieged at Preston. Among the government troops surrounding the town were the Cameronians. And once again they found themselves on the right side of history, this time forcing the besieged to capitulate.

On the very same day, Mar and his army were at Sheriffmuir, near Dunblane. It was ground chosen by the smaller government force commanded by the Campbell Duke of Argyll, and even though they were outnumbered by two to one they managed to avoid defeat and stall Mar's advance. It was early winter and misty at Sheriffmuir. When the armies formed up in battle order the right wing of one was significantly extended beyond the left wing of the other. The effect was that when the Highlanders (on both sides) charged across the frosted grass the whole battle turned like a wheel. It was a shambles, a disordered ruck of pushing and shoving, and by the evening Mar decided to allow Argyll to withdraw while he himself retreated to Perth. A popular ballad summed up Sheriffmuir:

A battle there was that I saw, man.
And we ran, and they ran,
And they ran, and we ran,
And we ran, and they ran awa', man!

It was not the most encouraging prelude to the arrival of the rightful king. A few days before Christmas 1715 James VIII and III disembarked at Peterhead and began what he hoped was a triumphal progress through his kingdom of Scotland. The royal court was set up at Scone Palace, near Perth and a grand proclamation issued. On the ancient Hill of Faith, the site of the crowning and consecration of Scottish kings since Kenneth MacAlpin, James VIII of Scotland would formally accede to the throne. It never happened. Only 27 years old, raised in the frustrated neverland of the Stuart court in exile at Saint-Germain-en-Laye, near Paris, James was out of his depth in the Scottish winter, surrounded by clan chiefs and lowland noblemen he had never met and could barely understand. Shy, even cold and aloof, he failed to rally his supporters to him, to inspire or put steel in them. The charisma essential to make the return of the king succeed was sadly lacking and the plans for a coronation at Scone were quietly shelved. By the end of January government troops were regrouping and the garrison at Stirling was strengthened. And each night more and more clansmen slipped away, going home to their winter hearths. It was time to go. On 4 February James VIII took ship for France and as it sailed out of Montrose's vast harbour, the last realistic hope of a Stuart monarchy disappeared over the horizon.

Government reprisals were surprisingly but sensibly muted. Most of the aristo-cratic ringleaders of the rebellion forfeited their estates and two suffered the appalling deaths of traitors on London's Tower Hill. Mar managed to escape into exile and died in France in 1732. Difficult to enforce in remote areas, legislation was more nominal than effective. The Disarming Act and the Clan Act of 1716 attempted to inhibit the military nature of clan society and to continue to undermine its core relationships. Few in the Highlands paid much attention. A year later an Act of Grace pardoned all clansmen involved in the rising – except, of course, for the MacGregors.

Much more practical than the windy words of parliament was the work of an expe-rienced soldier:

ABOVE *James VIII and III, the king in exile.*

> Lord, grant that Marshal Wade
> May, by thy mighty aid,
> Victory bring.
> May he sedition hush
> And, like a torrent rush,
> Rebellious Scots to crush.
> God save the King.

So runs the sixth verse of the British national anthem, composed in the 1740s. Not often sung in Scotland now, or indeed anywhere else, it nevertheless shows with brutal clarity how central the defeat of Jacobitism was to a proper sense of Britishness, and how peripheral to it the Highland

clans were. Not even English speakers, they were outside the new united kingdom and a threat to it, a threat to be crushed.

George Wade was an unusual figure. Born in Ireland in 1673 he rose steadily through the ranks of the British army to become a Major-General and finally a Field Marshal. His close involvement in the suppression of the Jacobites in 1715 prompted George I's government to commission a report on the condition of Scotland, and in particular how the threat posed by the clans might be best dealt with. In 1724 he came north 'to inspect the present situation of the Highlanders' and 'make strict enquiry into the last law for disarming the Highlanders.'

Enforcement was the key. Parliament could pass all the laws it liked but if there were no credible means of enforcing them, then the clans would continue to act as they pleased. Roads were required, Wade realized, and a network of permanent garrisons to discourage rebellion and deal with local disturbances.

When he was appointed Commander in Chief of His Majesty's forces, castles, forts and barracks in North Britain Wade wasted no time in putting his proposals in hand. Between 1728 and 1730 a road was built to connect Perth with Inverness; the modern-day A9 follows it. It was a crucial military artery, making it possible for government troops to penetrate the heart of the country south of the Great Glen. Barracks were built beside the road at Ruthven, near Kingussie, and by 1740 all of the garrisons in the Highlands were linked. Soldiers, supplies and artillery could move quickly between Fort William, Fort Augustus, Fort George and Ruthven.

Bridges presented the most formidable logistical – and financial – challenge. Forty so-called Wade bridges were built and perhaps the most famous and elegant crosses the Tay at Aberfeldy. It was completed in 1734 and cost £4,000. Beside the approach to Aberfeldy bridge is another testament to Wade's busy acumen. It is a stone marking the founding of the Black Watch regiment. In 1724 the general raised a militia known as the Highland Watches as a means of policing the glens. There were at first three companies of Campbells, and one each of Frasers, Grants and Munros. Four more were recruited and by 1739 the regiment was known as *Am Freiceadan Dubh*, the Black Watch. Having fought in the British army with great courage at the Battle of Fontenoy (1743), the Highlanders were described as 'the Black Watch of the Battles, first to come and last to go'.

OPPOSITE *Field Marshall George Wade (1673–1748).*

Over three centuries the regiment acquired an unmatched reputation, winning 172 battle honours, more than any other regiment of foot. The Black Watch were also permitted to continue to wear the kilt at a time when it and any form of tartan were banned. Their particular sett of very dark blue, green and black quickly became a standard weave and it is probably the oldest in existence. It is known as the government tartan. A version was eventually adopted by Clan Campbell. As the first regular Highland regiment in the British army, the Black Watch began a long and distinguished tradition.

George II was curious. The fearsome military reputation of the clans intrigued him. A soldier himself, he wanted to understand what manner of men General Wade had gone to such pains and expense to contain. The king wanted to see for himself.

After making enquiries, royal agents sent messages to Gregor Drummond and his cousin, James, summoning them to a meeting in Perth. There the two clansmen were kidnapped, bundled into a coach and driven south to London with an escort. Gregor had been forced to take the name of Drummond because of the proscription of his clan. He was a MacGregor and most knew him as Griogair Boidheach, Gregor the Beautiful. Tall and very good looking, he was also reckoned by the chiefs and the men of the southern clans to be a great warrior, perhaps the greatest and most skilled of his time.

BELOW *The elegant Wade bridge at Aberfeldy.*

At St James' Palace, Gregor and James were taken under heavy guard into the central courtyard and each given a broadsword, the long, two-handed claymore. As George II looked down from the royal apartments, they put on a dazzling display of strength and swordsmanship. As the ring of mitred redcoats looked on nervously, Gregor and James exchanged the swords for double-bladed Lochaber axes and swung and threw them with mesmerizing skill.

Deeply impressed, George II had the two Highlanders ushered into his presence in a stateroom. Neither party spoke much English, but the king had each man given a golden guinea. Utterly affronted at the insult, saying that they fought for honour and not for money, Gregor and James stormed out and gave the golden guineas to the amazed flunkeys who opened the doors for them.

Three years later Gregor the Beautiful fought at Culloden, but it is not known if he survived. James fled to Paris where he attempted to capture and abduct the Jacobite agent, Allan Breck Stewart, a character later made famous by Robert Louis Stevenson.

On the morning of Monday 19 August 1745 a rowing boat was making its slow, stately way up Loch Shiel, heading for the foot of Glenfinnan. Through the clear summer air Colonel John O'Sullivan looked anxiously at the shoreline of the northern fringes of the loch. There seemed to be very few men waiting. The time of the rendezvous had been set for an hour after midday, but where were all the banners fluttering in the breeze? Where was the expectant press of men, the

LEFT *The Lochaber axe with its characteristic hook used to unseat cavalry by pulling at reins and tack.*

crowd straining to see? Beside O'Sullivan in the stern of the boat sat the man who would be king. Prince Charles Edward Stuart, the Young Pretender, the eldest son of King James VIII and III, would succeed to the thrones of Scotland, England and Ireland, and in the name of his father and his family, he had come home to reclaim his kingdom.

BELOW *Sir Donald Cameron, also known as Gentle Locheil, by Sir George Chalmers, 1762.*

The great enterprise had not begun well. After the Scottish banker, Aeneas MacDonald, had raised loans in Paris on the security of Queen Clementina's, Prince Charles' mother's, jewelry, Charles' agents had bought arms and artillery and hired two ships to take him and a brigade of 800 exiled Scots and Irish soldiers to Scotland. One ship was attacked and forced to turn back, while the other had landed the Prince on the island of Eriskay on 23 July. Two influential clan chiefs on nearby Skye, Alexander MacDonald of Sleat and Norman MacLeod of Dunvegan, had refused to meet him and when Charles arrived on the mainland near Arisaig others had advised him to abandon the expedition. He had not brought enough men or supplies, and where were the French?

As the rowing boat drew nearer to the loch shore, O'Sullivan's heart sank when he counted only 50 or so men waiting. It was embarrassing, their worst fears realized, and the ignominy of an immediate return to France loomed. Even when Allan MacDonald of Morar emerged from the woodland around the western trail at the head of 150 more clansmen, it was still no more than an escort and very far indeed from an army.

Around the middle of the afternoon, from somewhere to the north, came the sound that changed everything. Floating clear above the trees of Glenfinnan the skirl of the pipes turned every head. It seemed to come from the top of the narrow valley, the flanks of the ridge of Sgurr Thuilm. Men recognized the music. Thanks be to the Lord. Clan Cameron had come.

The sharp eyed could make out lines of clansmen snaking down the tracks on the mountainside. Maybe a thousand! Maybe more! At last, these were the makings of an army. Sir John MacDonald remembered the immense relief:

> Never have I seen anything so quaintly pleasing as the march of this troop of Highlanders as they descended a steep mountain by a zig-zag path.

Led by Sir Donald Cameron of Locheil, who had at first advised Prince Charles to return to France and then changed his mind, there were 700 Camerons and 300 MacDonalds of Keppoch. When they had mustered by the shores of the loch and the Prince had greeted Locheil warmly, the royal party and the chiefs climbed the low hill by the stream that runs through the glen. After the Marquis of Tullibardine had drawn up in ranks the men of the Jacobite army, Prince Charles and his equerries unfurled the scarlet and white silk standard of the Stuarts, and he then proclaimed his father rightful king of Scotland, England and Ireland. Few of those listening would have understood. The Prince had no Gaelic and probably spoke in French, but there was evidently a translator on hand.

Soon after the proclamation, more clansmen came to Glenfinnan, and this time they brought English prisoners. Three hundred MacDonells of Glengarry had ambushed a company of redcoats in the Great Glen, near Spean Bridge, and had taken a Captain Swettenham captive. He proved invaluable to the cause. After extracting the romantic promise that he would desist from fighting the Jacobites or their supporters for a year and a day, Swettenham was allowed to go free. John O'Sullivan recorded:

> This officer behaved very gallantly, he frightened the governors of those garrisons he passed by, and even [General] Cope. For he told them all that the Prince had 6,000 men, and that neither arms nor money was wanting to them: he gave everywhere the most favourable account that could be given of the Prince's activity and person. It is said the Elector [George II] sent for him when he arrived in London, and asked him what kind of a man the Prince was, [and] he answered that he was as fine a figure, as clever a Prince as a man could set eyes on, upon which George turned his back and left him there.

In an age without rapid or mass communication, witnesses like Swettenham were avidly listened to and believed. And almost before it began in earnest, the 1745 Rebellion had already acquired an air of glamour.

ABOVE *The Marquis of Tullibardine.*

The Prince led his army south and more of the clans rose to support him. The pattern of recruitment was never uniform, or even predictable. Clans split their loyalties and families were sometimes divided – none more so than that of the chief of the Mackintoshes. When he opted to take command of a government militia for George II his young wife declared for Prince Charles. Lady Anne became known as Colonel Anne as she raised the clan for the Stuarts. Only 20 years old and said to be very

ABOVE *Prince Charles at Loch nan Uamh with Antoine Walsh who had brought him from Eriskay.*

beautiful, she rode the Mackintosh glens, and either by sweet cajolement or threat, pinned the white cockades on her men with her own hand. When Colonel Anne brought her clan to the Prince, much later in the campaign, she wore a tartan riding habit and a man's blue bonnet to catch up her long hair.

By the end of August the rebels had taken Perth unopposed and the Prince had been joined by the Atholl Brigade and Lord George Murray, the younger brother of the Duke of Perth. He was an experienced and capable commander, but the charms of the young Prince appear to have grated from the first. A crucial relationship, it was thought to be cold and argumentative. Had the two men been close, things might have fallen out very differently. James Johnstone, an exile who had returned to fight in the Jacobite army, echoed a common belief when he later wrote:

> Had Prince Charles slept during the whole of the expedition, and allowed Lord George to act for him, according to his own judgement, there is every reason for supposing he would have found the crown of Great Britain on his head when he awoke.

General Sir John Cope commanded the government army in Scotland and it had probably been his intention to confront the clans in the Highlands and to try to contain the rebellion in the north. But the speed and direction of enemy advance as well as a lack of good intelligence left Cope little option but to march to Aberdeen and ship his army south. Meanwhile the Jacobites aimed for Edinburgh and its royal palace.

In common with most of urban and central Scotland, Edinburgh stayed loyal to the Hanoverians, but at the approach of the rebel army the defenders of the city proved hilariously useless. When flanking Jacobite cavalry encountered a force of government dragoons at Coltbridge, to the west of the city, near Roseburn, there was a rout. In what was called *The Canter of Coltbrig* the soldiers simply fled for their lives. One of the rebel commanders, Lord Elcho, recalled what happened next:

> At 8 o'clock at night the Prince sent a message to the magistrates of Edinburgh to demand the keys of the town and to tell them he intended to enter it either that night or the next day, and if there was any resistance made, whoever was found in arms should be severely treated; and besides, he could not answer but if the town was taken by storm his soldiers would plunder it. At ten at night there came four of the town council out to the Prince's quarters to beg if he would give them time to think on his demand. This was a message contrived to gain time, for they expected General Cope's army every hour to land at Leith

from Aberdeen, and in case he landed time enough, they intended to wait the event of a battle. The Prince, after they had kissed his hand, told them that he was going to send a detachment to attack the town and let them defend it at their peril; that if they did the consequences would be bad, and if they did not he intended no harm to the old metropolis of his kingdom. As soon as they received this answer the Prince ordered Young Locheil with 800 men to march and attack the town. There came out sometime after another deputation of six councillors; Provost Coutts was one of them. They got the same answer as the first, and the Prince would not see them. The coach that they came out in went in at the West Port and set down the company, and as they were letting out the coach at the Netherbow, Locheil's party who were arrived there rushed in, seized all the guards of the town, who made no resistance, and made themselves masters of Edinburgh without firing a shot.

There had been very few guards to seize at the Netherbow Port because Edinburgh's Defence Volunteers had almost all melted away. On 15 September 400 men had mustered in the morning, but when they were ordered to march out and confront the Highland army, 358 of them suddenly remembered more pressing business. Among the stubborn remnant stood a young David Hume. The great philosopher and historian showed real courage, willing to risk his life for his convictions and to take part in history as well as write about it.

The Jacobite army did not have long to enjoy their easy victory. Provost Coutts had been frantically playing for time because the fleet carrying General Sir John Cope's army had been sighted at the mouth of the Firth of Forth. In the event they disembarked at Dunbar on 17 September. Having quickly marched along the coast road, they formed up in battle order near Prestonpans and waited for the Highlanders. Expecting an attack from the west, Cope had chosen his ground well with protection on one side from a stone dyke and an impassable bog on the other. In front lay a ditch that would blunt the much-feared charge of the clansmen.

But nothing went to plan. From an East Lothian Jacobite, Robert Anderson, Lord George Murray learned that there was a secret path through the impenetrable bog. At dead of night, in complete silence, he led his Highland regiments through and had them form up on the eastern side of the government forces where the ground was much better. When dawn broke and General Cope peered through the grey light he was thunderstruck to see an entire army behind him, 'looking like a black hedge moving towards us.'

Cope swung his inexperienced troops around just as Clan Cameron broke into the charge, racing towards the disordered lines of redcoats. It was a misty morning and many clansmen seemed to scream out of nothing, roaring their war cries. Their broadswords raised high, they tore into Cope's terrified troops.

The Battle of Prestonpans lasted only 15 minutes. As the clansmen swung their Lochaber axes and slashed with their claymores, the redcoats broke and ran for their lives. But many were killed, perhaps 500, in the ferocious momentum of the first onslaught. Prince Charles galloped about the battlefield imploring his soldiers to stop the slaughter, shouting that the government men were also his father's subjects. It was no use. The Highlanders understood only Gaelic and thought their commander-in-chief was inciting them to greater efforts.

Contemporary English commentators were outraged at what happened at Prestonpans:

> [They] were killed in cold blood – the foot seeing themselves as naked and defenceless, and the enemy rushing impetuously upon them, sword in hand, they threw down their arms and surrendered as prisoners. But the merciless enemy would grant no quarters until they were compelled by their superior officers. The unheard of manner in which the dead were mangled and the wounded disfigured was the great evidence of the truth of this.

British army surgeons added:

> …never saw such terrible gashes as the Highlanders made with their broadswords.

These and other observations all added to a sense of the Highlanders as a force of nature, an atavism, sub-humans who could mete out savage treatment – and therefore expect nothing else in return. After Culloden the savages who had cut a government army to pieces were themselves to suffer a concerted campaign of appalling savagery.

After waiting too long in Edinburgh for more recruits and more encouragement from Louis XV of France, the Jacobite army invaded England. Avoiding General Wade's forces at Newcastle, they marched down the western roads to Preston and beyond. Prince Charles had good reason to hope for a French invasion across the Channel, and if he could make a dash for London, George II and his generals might have to defend the capital on two fronts.

By 4 December the rebels had entered Derby, only 127 miles from London. But there were serious problems. Few recruits had joined the

Jacobite army in England and with the winter closing in, a French invasion looked less and less likely. And Lord George Murray and the Prince were barely on speaking terms. The council of war decided on retreat to Scotland, and with Charles sulking and refusing to be involved, Lord George conducted a brilliant rearguard campaign, extracting the army from hostile territory virtually intact. But the Jacobites had taken the first weary steps on the road to Culloden and the extinction of their cause.

When the smoke cleared on Drummossie Moor on 16 April 1746 the government cavalry chased and rode down the fleeing Highland army. Their fury was indiscriminate. In an appalling aftermath, troopers swung their sabres at every man, woman and child they encountered. The schoolboys in the heather were discovered and attacked, and on the road to Inverness people who had not been involved in the fighting were chased and often killed or horribly wounded.

On the battlefield the carnage was pitiful. Many clansmen lay wounded, immobilized, and they were bayoneted or shot. General Henry Hawley, whose troops had fled from the Jacobite army at Falkirk only three months before, rode among the dead and dying, pointing out stirrings of life with his

BELOW *An idealized but beautifully composed version of Prince Charles' triumphant entry into Edinburgh in 1745.*

ABOVE *Flora MacDonald (1722–90)*
wearing the white roses of the Jacobite cause.

staff, shouting to his men to run and bayonet their enemies again and again, just to be sure. Pinned by the bodies of his dead clansmen, Charles Fraser of Inverallochie was found to be alive and is said to have turned up his blood-covered face to glare silently at Hawley before a redcoat ran up and killed him.

Some men fought to beyond the end of their strength and courage. One of the few Highlanders to break through the government lines was Gillies MacBean, a major in the Clan Chattan regiment. Before his leg was broken by grapeshot he had killed 14 men, but when his clan retreated MacBean could not stay with them. Dragoons caught up with the wounded man by a drystane dyke. Surrounded, he backed against the wall and summoning up every last shred of his immense strength, the clansman fought like a man possessed. The dragoons had to spur their horses forward to trample him under their thrashing hoofs. Watching the fight, Lord Ancrum shouted that MacBean should be spared but in their murderous intensity his men ignored him. But still he was not dead. After the government soldiers wheeled away, their attention elsewhere, MacBean crawled to a barn on a nearby croft. Hidden under straw by an old woman, his terrible wounds finally overcame his astonishing bravery.

Meanwhile Prince Charles fled into hiding. With a price of £30,000 on his head he could have been betrayed at any time and was forced to keep moving, taking a zig-zag route through the northern Highlands to the Atlantic coast. Companies of soldiers everywhere searched for the fugitive while most of their comrades marched down the Great Glen. The killing and plundering went on, and this time the clans were certainly disarmed. The redcoats were thorough. Here is an extract from a letter to friends in London from a captain of dragoons:

> We have been dismounted these past two months and taken a great many rebels, both in the Highlands and Lowlands; numbers refused to surrender which has caused many skirmishes wherein several of the rebels have been killed. We seize and divide all their goods and cattle, which is distributed among the private men by order of His Royal Highness [the Duke of Cumberland] who by his conduct has rendered himself the bravest and best of generals.

The lands of the clans deeply involved in the rebellion were attacked and looted. When soldiers could capture what they called 'rebel bitches' women were raped repeatedly and then forced to watch the murder of their fathers, husbands and sons. If lookouts saw a column of redcoats approaching whole communities did not hesitate to flee. Ranald MacDonald of Keppoch was only seven years old but he later recalled what happened:

> *After the battle of Culloden the cruelty of the soldiers made us fly from our homes; and the first night we went and drove all our cows and sheep about two miles from the house and carried all our provisions upon the horses, our bed-clothes, and all the other goods in the house to the place where we took our night's lodgings, and pulled ling to make a fire and bed of, and we laid beside a little water that was at the bottom of two hills.*

Prince Charles also found himself occasionally sleeping in the heather, evading capture, sometimes by narrow margins. Having grown a beard, he spent a week with an outlaw group known as the Seven Men of Glenmoriston. After Culloden some clansmen had formed themselves into small bands who lived wild and sustained themselves by cattle reiving and theft. They well knew what certain fate awaited if they returned to their homes and families. The Seven Men lived in a great cave at the head of Glenmoriston with a stream running through its gravel floor. At the end of July 1746 they sheltered the fugitive Prince for a week. Soon after he moved on they showed great skill and courage when they held off a company of 100 government soldiers. The Seven Men stayed together for several years, but the winters in the cave must have been hard.

The romance of the flight of the Prince was much enhanced by his meeting with Flora MacDonald. The daughter of a tacksman on South Uist, she was visiting her brother on the island in June 1746. It was overrun by government soldiers searching for Prince Charles, and his capture seemed inevitable. Perhaps persuaded by the Chief of Clan Ranald, Flora became involved in what she called 'a fantastical scheme' to help Charles escape to Skye. Dressed in a blue and white frock and disguised as 'Betty Burke, an Irish girl', and supposedly Flora's maid, the Prince abandoned all his dignity and boarded a ship in Benbecula bound for Waternish in Skye. Almost inter-cepted by government troops, they nevertheless managed to make landfall and crossed the island to Portree, where they parted.

When the details of the dramatic episode became known, Flora MacDonald was arrested and imprisoned in the Tower of London. Several of the chiefs and leaders involved in the rebellion were fellow prisoners and some were executed, but, with the passage of the Act of Indemnity in 1747, Flora was released.

By 13 September 1746 French frigates were at last sighted in Loch nan Uamh, a sea-loch near Arisaig. It was the place where Prince Charles had landed 14 months before. With Cameron of Locheil and a handful of others, he boarded and sailed away to ponder what might have been.

There can be no doubt that the London government was extremely and repeatedly lucky. The Jacobite rebellions were not predestined to fail, and if bad weather had not prevented a French invasion – on several occasions – the Stuarts might have regained the throne. As it was Prince Charles was to spend 43 years in exile, closely watched by British agents. As he descended into obesity and alcoholism, the threat diminished. In 1780 Charles had set up his court in Italy, in the Palazzo Guagdini in Florence, and the British ambassador, Sir Horace Mann, reported that domestic violence had broken out. After Prince Charles (now King Charles after the death of his father) had attacked his wife, a German aristocrat, Louise de Stolberg-Gedern, she had fled for sanctuary to a nearby convent in the Via de Mandorlo. The King of Britain and Ireland was enraged, banged on the door and demanded to be let in to see his wife. The abbess refused, and Charles III stood in the street, screaming abuse, waking the neighbours.

It was a sad end to many old songs, tragedy ending in farce.

8

LOCHABER NO MORE

An ataireachd bhuan,
Cluinn fuaim na h'ataireachd
ard.
Tha torann a'chuain
Mar chualas leam-s' 'nam phaisd.
Gun mhuthadh, gun truas
A' sluaisreadh gainneimh na
tragh'd.
An ataireachd bhuan,
Cluinn fuaim na h'ataireachd
ard.

Sna coilltean a siar,
Chan iarrain fuireach gu brath.
Bha m'intinn 's mo mhiann
A riamh air lagan a' bhaigh.
Ach iadsan bha fial
An gniomh, an caidreamh 's
an agh
Air scapadh gun dion
Mar thriallas ealtainn roimh
namh…

The eternal surge of the sea,
Listen to the roar of the mighty
surge.
The thundering of the ocean is
As I heard it in my childhood,
Without cease, without pity,
Washing over the sands of the
shore.
The eternal surge of the sea,
Listen to the roar of the mighty
surge.

In the woods of the west,
I would not want to wait forever.
My mind and my longing
Were ever in the little hollow by
the cove.
But those who were gracious
In action, in friendship and in
laughter
Are scattered without protection
Like a flock of birds before an
enemy…

OPPOSITE Lochaber No More *by John Watson Nicol, 1883.*

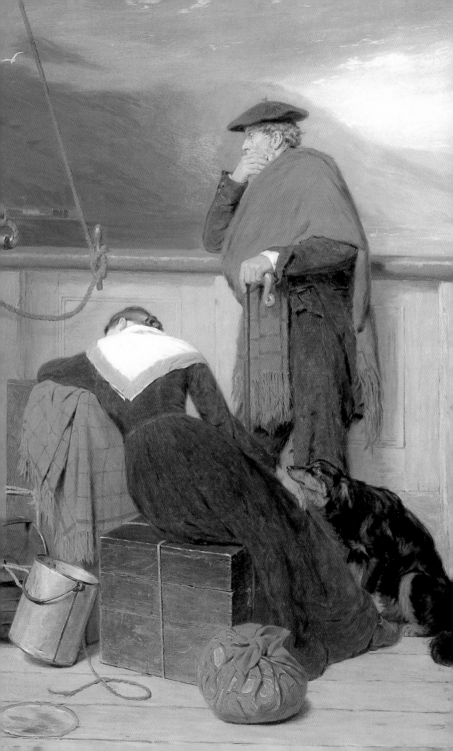

A schoolteacher on the Isle of Lewis, Donald MacIver, visited the deserted township of Carnish on a summer Sunday afternoon in the 1890s. With him was his uncle, Domhnall Ban Crosd. An old man by then, he had been a child when the Carnish families had been cleared off the land in 1851 and, like many, he had sailed soon after to a new life in Canada. When Domhnall Ban saw his birthplace again he wept and said, 'Chaneil nith an seo man a bha e, ach an ataireachd na mara', there is nothing here now as it was, except for the surge of the sea.

Overwhelmed by the old man's sadness and sense of loss, MacIver wrote his great lyric, also one of the most beautiful of Gaelic songs, a poem to the pain of leaving. For the two centuries after Culloden departure was the dominant theme of Highland history.

The clans had been broken. After the morning of 15 April 1746 they ceased almost at once to be politically significant. And like a flock of birds before an enemy, they began to scatter and the landscape emptied. Using Wade's roads, bridges and fortresses, the Duke of Cumberland's army ruthlessly and rigorously enforced the new Disarming Act. Thirty major clans, from almost every part of the Highlands except Argyll, came out for the Prince and their lands were attacked, their chiefs driven into exile, executed or impoverished. The Campbells and the other Hanoverian clans compounded organized government suppression by raiding into Cameron, MacDonald and Jacobite clan territories. Heritable jurisdiction, the right of chiefs to act as judges for their clansmen and women, was summarily abolished and the Episcopalian church in Scotland was persecuted. Tartan, the kilt and bagpipes were banned as the lineaments and instruments of war, and hundreds of clansmen who escaped the hangman's noose were herded on to transport ships for the colonies. As the fell consequences of military disaster settled like dark clouds over the mountains, morale drained away and the independent spirit of the clans and their chiefs shrivelled and died. After Culloden the clans were broken. The woods of the west grew wild once more, and by the shore houses were left deserted and all that remained was the high surge of the sea.

Only a generation after Culloden two entirely different versions of Highland history and culture began to take shape, one almost oblivious of the other, despite both existing in parallel in the same country. The dark realities of continuing repression and the beginnings of mass emigration ran alongside the invention of a dream of the Highlands and the subsequent wholesale adoption of the iconography of the clans by Lowland Scotland.

The dream began to stir in 1760 when the Scottish poet, James MacPherson, published *Fragments of Ancient Poetry Collected in the Highlands of Scotland*. Translated into English, these purported to be written versions of very old oral works collected from clan bards. A year later MacPherson claimed to have discovered a lost epic poem on the tales of Fingal, a great Celtic hero, composed by a Homeric figure known as Ossian. *The Works of Ossian* were a publishing sensation, a bestseller enjoying widespread European success. Goethe was inspired and throughout his campaigns Napoleon kept a copy of Ossian by him. Homeric in scale as well as inspiration, mysterious in origin, the poems recast the Highlands in a new heroic light. Barbarous incivility was replaced by the elemental grandeur of misty mountains and remote glens peopled by noble savages. Epic poetry was found to have been made among epic scenery.

Dr Samuel Johnson dismissed MacPherson's work as romantic fakery and also bad verse. He was asked 'But Dr Johnson, do you really believe that any

BELOW The Last of the Clans *by Thomas Faed, 1865.*

man today could write such poetry?' and replied, 'Yes. Many men. Many women. And many children.' But Ossian nevertheless set a tone, one which has persisted and which clothed the Highlands in attractive aura. Now that the military threat of the people of the misty glens had been safely neutralized, Lowlanders and others could begin to imagine a northern neverland. For all of the interest, the valuable contribution of millions of visitors, Highlanders have good reason to be grateful to James MacPherson.

The controversy over the authenticity of Ossian and the other poetry was not resolved until 1952. An eminent Gaelic scholar, Derick Thomson, concluded convincingly that while some of the material was indeed very old and clearly formed part of a long oral tradition, much was also invented and reorganized by MacPherson himself. Nevertheless what people believed was what mattered and with the publication of Ossian the romance of the Highlands was born and it was to make some notable and influential converts.

Unsentimental reality began to empty the glens, especially of their young men. Sorely in need of troops to prosecute the Seven Years War against the French, the Prime Minister, William Pitt, encouraged the recruitment of two Highland regiments in 1757. Justifying the putting of arms into the hands of men who had rebelled against the crown only ten years before, Pitt wrote to the king:

> *I sought for merit wherever it was to be found. It is my boast that I was the first minister who looked for it and found it in the mountains of the north. I called it forth and drew into your service a hardy and intrepid race of men…they served with fidelity as they fought with valour and conquered for you in every part of the world.*

Two years later General James Wolfe attacked Quebec, sent the Fraser Highlanders to scale the Heights of Abraham and defeated the army of the French general, Montcalm. The battle saw what may have been the last Highland charge. Wolfe had fought at Culloden and, echoing Pitt, took a cynical view of his new recruits: 'The Highlanders are hardy, intrepid, accustomed to rough country, and it is no great mischief if they fall. How can you better employ a secret enemy than by making his end conducive to the common good?' Back in London Pitt defended what seemed like a foolhardy gamble on the brutal basis that 'not many of them will return.'

OPPOSITE *Jean-Auguste-Dominique Ingres,* Ossian's Dream, *1813. Dreams of a heroic, mythic Highland past, oddly Greek and Roman in atmosphere.*

As the Fraser Highlanders climbed the sheer river cliffs above the St Lawrence, one of their captains was killed by musket shot. He was Simon Fraser of Inverallochie, the son of Charles Fraser who had been killed in cold blood at Culloden on the orders of General Henry Hawley. Even after the rebellion and its savage recriminations, Highlanders continued to pay a blood price. It is estimated that 12,000 clansmen fought in the Seven Years War and that between 1756 and 1815 a total of at least 40,000, perhaps as many as 75,000, were recruited into the British army in the great drive for empire. In all there were 24 Highland regiments of the line and 26 fencibles, that is, soldiers bound only for home postings. It is a vast number, especially when compared to estimates of the population of the Highlands. In 1755 there were probably 115,000 living north of the Highland Line, rising to 154,000 by 1801. Wolfe was right: much of the British Empire was bought by the blood of the clans and peace in their native place guaranteed by its shedding.

Not all were cannon fodder. Some Highland soldiers led truly remarkable lives, fighting in far-flung places, carving out unexpected niches in history. Few were more exotic than Sir Gregor MacGregor. Born on Christmas Eve 1786 in Queen Street in Edinburgh, Gregor was one of the first male children to bear his right name for 175 years. Ten years before, the proscription of the name of Clan Gregor had at last been lifted. But resentments had not died. Gregor was the grandson of Gregor the Beautiful and his father and nurse told the boy the story of his clan, and inspired him to the life of a soldier.

In 1810 the young man found himself in the British Army, under the command of Sir Arthur Wellesley, later to become the Duke of Wellington. MacGregor fought with such bravery in the campaigns in Portugal and Spain that he was promoted by Wellesley and knighted by the King of Spain. Allegedly. It was said that a glittering military career awaited, but the young officer had other ideas. The agents of Simón Bolívar recruited MacGregor to join the great liberator in the wars against Spain in South America. Eventually the young Highlander became Commandant General of the Cavalry in the Army of the Republic of Venezuela, and he married Bolívar's niece, the beautiful Dona Josefa.

After various adventures as a mercenary, MacGregor conceived an astonishing plan, perhaps one of the greatest confidence tricks ever perpetrated. He invented a country. Having come to an arrangement, over a bottle of whisky, with the chief of the Miskito Indians of Central America,

MacGregor took ship for Britain. By the time he disembarked, he had become His Serene Highness Gregor I, Prince of Poyais. It was 1820 and George IV was the new king. When he offered to present his credentials at the Court of St James, where his grandfather had been insulted to be given a golden guinea, the Prince of Poyais was delighted when George IV agreed to see him. It was exactly the sort of immediate credibility MacGregor needed for the next part of his plan to succeed.

Brochures were printed. They spoke of a land in the Americas ripe for exploitation. It was rich in timber, thousands of head of cattle grazed its plains, fruit trees bloomed and there were hints of 'very many gold mines.' MacGregor hit on the idea of printing Poyais banknotes. Presses in Edinburgh turned out the only Gaelic currency ever made, for on it MacGregor had printed the motto of Clan Gregor, 'S Rioghal mo Dhream. Appropriately for His Serene Highness it translates as 'My Race is Royal'.

There was hysteria and people clamoured to buy shares/banknotes and soon an expedition to Poyais was fitted out. When the ships reached their destination they found not a land of milk and honey, not the promised Poyais, but what has become known as the Mosquito Coast. Swamps, jungle and deadly disease awaited those gullible souls who had believed the brochure's claims. Gold mines were nowhere to be seen and instead of fertile plains and fruit trees impenetrable rain forest stretched as far as the eye could see. When the deception was exposed MacGregor was arrested, spent a little time in prison, escaped and made his way back to South America. As a hero of the liberation, Venezuela welcomed him, granted MacGregor a generous pension and a spacious villa overlooking the Caribbean. As he sipped a drink on the verandah MacGregor may have reflected on a brilliant confidence trick, and that for once a Highlander had been the exploiter and not the exploited.

Exploitation had been gathering pace in the second half of the 18th century. Often led by their tacksmen, more than 20,000 clansmen, women and children left the Highlands between 1763 and 1775. Many sailed across the Atlantic for the Americas and a new way of life. Others turned south to industrializing Clydeside and Glasgow became home to a large Gaelic-speaking community. By 1836 there were thought to be at least 22,000 living in the tenements.

In 1773 the enemy of Ossian and James MacPherson, Dr Samuel Johnson, came north to see for himself. Accompanied by James Boswell he took care to listen and observe:

There was perhaps never any change of national manners so quick, so great and so general as that which has operated in the Highlands by the late conquest and subsequent laws…The clans retain little now of their original character. Their ferocity of temper is softened, their military ardour is extinguished, their contempt for government subdued and their reverence for their chiefs abated.

Johnson saw that the old clan chiefs, 'the patriarchal rulers', had quickly become what he condemned as 'rapacious landlords' anxious to begin 'turning their estates to the best advantage'. It had happened before. When the Border Reivers were finally tamed in the early 17th century many of their heidsmen, the leaders of their surnames, had turned against their own people, evicting them, compiling great estates from their tenancies and becoming ruthless landlords. They took the side of the state, of order against lawlessness and, ignoring their own misdemeanors, used the law to part their people from their land. In the Highlands many of the chiefs broke the old bonds of *dùthchas*, and if their clansmen, and especially the women, attempted to stand in the way of profit and progress they could be swept off the land, down to the sea and the waiting

ships. A Mackenzie bard wept as he composed his last lyric:

I see the hills, the valleys and the slopes,
But they do not lighten my sorrow.
I see the bands departing
On the white-sailed ships.
I see the Gael rising from his door.
I see the people going,
And there is no love for them in the north.

Sheep were more profitable than people and 1792 became known as *Am Bliadhna nan Caorach*, the Year of the Sheep. Much bigger and as hardy as the native breed, large herds of Cheviots were shipped from the south. Despite protests, especially in Ross and Sutherland, people were cleared off the land and replaced with the new herds. A bard of Clan Chisholm made a simple point:

The FIRST LAIRD in AW SCOTIA——or A VIEW at EDINBURGH in August, 1822.

"*O' my Bonny Bonny Highland Laddie; my Handsome, Charming, Highland Laddie.*"

Published Sept. 3, 1822, by JOHN FAIRBURN, Broadway, Ludgate Hill.

ABOVE *The visit of George IV to Edinburgh in 1822 drew merciless caricature.*
OPPOSITE *Armed to the teeth, a Highland soldier makes his way through rough country.*

Our chief has lost his feeling of kinship, he prefers sheep in the glen and his young men in the Highland Regiments.

While the harshness of recent history was felt all too keenly in the glens, much further south, in the Borders, the Jacobite rebellion produced a quite different effect. It stirred the imagination of Sir Walter Scott and was the inspiration for the first of his wildly successful historical novels. *Waverley* was published in 1814 and subtitled ''Tis Sixty Years Since', since the rebellion, he meant.

Scott had made his name with a series of long poems partly drawn from the imagery of Ossian. *The Lay of the Last Minstrel* and *The Lady of the Lake* sold widely and brought visitors north, the first literary tourists, especially to the Trossachs. *Waverley* was a departure for Scott, the first true historical novel. And of course it romanticized the rebellion and its major protagonists – and since it was the world's first international bestseller, it exerted a tremendously powerful influence on the way the middle and upper classes saw the Jacobites and their adherents. Romance swirled around the misty mountains once more.

What helped make Scott's version of Highland history and culture hard to shift was an extraordinary event that took place in 1822. It was decided that George IV would make a state visit to Scotland, the first reigning monarch to come north since Charles II. And because Scott's novels had by that time made him the most famous living Scotsman in the world he was asked to stage manage the event. What happened was jaw-dropping.

It seemed that most of Edinburgh's population gathered at the port of Leith to witness a remarkable sight. In August 1822 the traditionally built George IV stepped ashore and proceeded to spend two weeks at the centre of a tartan extravaganza. Persuaded by Scott into a Royal Stewart kilt worn several inches above the knee over flesh-coloured tights, the red-faced king reeled and strathspeyed his way through parties and balls at Holyrood Palace. 'Since he is here for such a short time,' remarked one witty Edinburgh lady, 'it is as well that we see so much of him.' The last royal visitor to Holyrood had arrived in 1745 with 6,000 clansmen at his back, and Prince Charles would have gasped at the behaviour of his great enemy's grandson as he puffed and perspired under bonnet, plaid and kilt. Had the world turned upside down? Scott's son-in-law, J. G. Lockhart, certainly thought so, [we] 'appear to be a nation of Highlanders, and the bagpipe and the tartan are the order of the day.'

There was momentum behind the strange events of 1822. An expatriate club, the Highland Society of London, had written to each of the clan chiefs in 1815 asking them to send a sample of their clan tartan to be deposited and registered. To many this was a baffling request since they had no idea that any such thing existed. But tartan manufacturers were often happy to supply a pattern (many were simply numbered or carried a place name for identification) for them to adopt and many so-called ancient or traditional setts date from this time. Following the pantomime of George IV's state visit the popularity of tartan surged tremendously and the notion that the particular surnames had some sort of right to particular patterns added a unique marketing twist. This was further developed by the entertaining Sobieski-Stewart brothers, John and Charles Edward. Claiming to be descendants of Bonnie Prince Charlie (as Prince Charles had tellingly become known), they compiled an allegedly ancient list of clan tartans in a book with the sonorous and serious title of *Vestiarium Scoticum*. Clearly bogus, widely trusted and much consulted, it is the origin of many of today's so-called clan setts.

Real Highlanders were more concerned with survival than setts. The potato had been successfully introduced and by 1780 was grown by almost every household. But, as in Ireland, a terrible blight took hold of the crop in the early 1840s and, although famine was averted, the disaster prompted another wave of emigration. Between 1847 and 1858 it is reckoned that 16,000 Highlanders left for the Americas or Australia. There were forced evictions in Barra, Lewis and the Uists, and sometimes men were tied up by the constables and forced to the quaysides and the white-sailed ships.

BELOW *Evictions recorded by a 19th-century photographer.*

Catherine MacPhee's memories of that terrible time were recorded in the 1870s. Here is a translation:

> *Many a thing have I seen in my own day…many a thing, oh Mary Mother… I have seen the townships swept and the big holdings being made of them, the people being driven out of the countryside to the streets of Glasgow and the wilds of Canada, such of them as did not die of hunger and plague and small-pox while going across the ocean. I have seen the women putting the children in the carts which were being sent from Benbecula and Iochdar to Lochboisdale, while their husbands lay bound in the pen and were weeping beside them, without power to give them a helping hand, though the women themselves were crying aloud and their little children wailing like to break their hearts. I have seen the big, strong men, the champions of the countryside, the stalwarts of the world, being bound on Lochboisdale quay and cast into the ship as would be done to a batch of horses or cattle in the boat, the bailiffs and the ground-officers and the constables gathered behind them in pursuit of them. The God of Life, and He only, knows all the loathsome work of men on that day.*

Queen Victoria of course saw none of this. When she and Prince Albert first came to the Highlands in 1842 they stayed at Drummond Castle as guests of the Earl of Breadalbane. Five years later, with Scott's romantic poetry at her elbow, the queen and her consort cruised up the Atlantic coastline in a yacht. It never stopped raining. Not discouraged, the royal couple had heard that the eastern Highlands were much drier and the weather generally kinder. They set about looking for a house.

Historical ironies abounded when they found one. Balmoral had belonged to the Farquharsons of Inverey, a clan who had fought bravely for the Prince at Culloden, and the house stands not far from the Braes of Mar, the place where the Jacobite standard was raised in rebellion against Victoria's ancestors in 1715.

The old Balmoral was demolished and a suitably grand mansion built in its place. Turrets, battlements and a keep-like tower announced a splendid and influential example of the Scottish baronial style of architecture and inside tartan was everywhere. On the floors, furnishing and curtains: Royal Stewart was the preferred sett. A century after Culloden and at the time of a second, brutal wave of Highland Clearance little could stand in the way of romance. Queen Victoria baffled historians when she claimed, more than once, that in her heart she was a Jacobite.

Balmoral had a tremendous impact. After 1855 the queen arrived there every August to spend several leisurely weeks in her beloved Highlands. Prime Ministers, cabinet ministers, civil servants and courtiers were obliged to follow her into the glens. And where Victoria led, high society most certainly followed. Hunting lodges in the Highlands were built for many aristocrats and wealthy businessmen. Many were keen deerstalkers (even inventing a hat favoured by Sherlock Holmes) and again the royal couple set an example. When he stayed with the Earl of Breadalbane in Perthshire, Prince Albert had shot two stags, and a long-standing trend was set. With the development of powerful and accurate rifles, so-called sporting estates were established, and by the time of the First World War several million acres were devoted to deer rather than people.

Those unable to run to guns, lodges and land also came north. Queen Victoria's love of the Highlands coincided with the railway building boom: lines reached Inverness in 1863 and Oban in 1880. Tourism was much encouraged by the enormous success of *Leaves from the Journal of our Life in the*

Highlands. Published in 1868, this was a digest of the queen's diaries and it talks of a very attractive and of course privileged series of holidays:

> *I cannot describe all we saw. But we saw where the Dee rises between the mountains…and such magnificent wild rocks, precipices and corries, most splendid. It had a sublime and solemn effect; so solitary, so wild, so severe, no-one but ourselves and our little party there.*
>
> *Albert went on further with the children, but I returned with Grant to my seat on the cairn, as I could not scramble about well. Soon after we all began walking and looking for 'cairn-gorms', of which we found some small ones. The mist had entirely cleared away below, so that we saw all the beautiful views. Ben Muich Duie is 4,297 feet high and the highest mountain in Scotland. I and Alice rode part of the way, but the steepest we walked, and then got on again – Albert and Bertie walked it. I had a little whisky and water again, as the people declared pure water would be too chilling.*

Victoria neatly summed up the principal attraction of the Highlands for the last 150 years: a splendid, epic emptiness. After Culloden and the Clearances a working landscape had degenerated into mere scenery, and to many the 'Monarch of the Glen' was no longer a clan chief but a stag crowned by twelve point antlers.

But there was whisky – to keep out the chill on the flanks of Ben MacDui (almost the highest mountain in Scotland). Derived from the Gaelic *uisge-beatha*, the water of life, it was mass produced for the first time in the 19th century. Commercial distillers realized that the best method of ensuring a consistent product was to blend malted whiskies with colourless, character-less but powerful grain whiskies. It also made bulk production easier. The largest manufacturers were all based in the Lowlands but the malt distilleries, always small-scale enterprises, have remained for the most part in the Highlands. Speyside has the greatest concentration but some particularly knowledgeable connoisseurs believe that the finest malt whisky is made in Campbelltown in Kintyre. Queen Victoria's fondness for the water of life did its popularity no harm and sales in the second half of the 19th century became very healthy.

Royal patronage encouraged another Highland institution. Games of various sorts had been held informally by chiefs and others for centuries,

OPPOSITE *A 19th-century painting of the Glengoyne Distillery near Killearn on the southern fringes of the Highlands.*

especially those involving manly feats of strength, but the Highland Games in their modern form are a 19th-century invention. Victoria and Albert began a royal tradition of supporting the Braemar Gathering and it features the classic competitions of tossing the caber, throwing the hammer and putting the weight. Tartan is of course everywhere and competitors are bound to wear kilts – except in foot racing. Highland clans and clan societies have taken to setting up small enclosures for their members at some events. These are very colourful at the Oban Highland Games with the Clan Campbell and Clan Stewart pennants flying.

The dancing competitions are genuinely old. Written records from the 16th century describe the famous sword dance where two swords are crossed on the ground and the dancer moves between each of the quarters without touching the sharp blades. Other forms recall specific political events. The *Seann Truibhas* (pron. Shawn Trooas) or the Old Trousers is a celebration of the repeal of the Proscription Act which banned the kilt after 1746. Clansmen were forced to wear trousers or trews, and when the dancer

BELOW *Pipe majors lead a massed pipe band in a Braemer Gathering in 2006.*
OVERLEAF *Throwing the hammer at a Highland Games in London in 1937.*

deliberately shakes each leg during the performance it symbolizes the shedding of the hated trousers. In the second part the dancer claps their hands and the piper increases the tempo. As the pleats swing and flick up, the joy of the return to the beautiful, elegant kilt is unmistakable.

Dances were the exclusive prerogative of men until the growth of Highland Games in the second half of the 19th century. There were no specific rules excluding women and when they began to enter they won prizes. Now, almost all competitors are female. Queen Victoria loved Highland dancing and eyebrows were raised and kilts buckled on as thousands of English aristocrats clearly understood that they were required to love it too.

Most of Victoria's reluctant reelers wore what is known in Gaelic as *am feile beag*, the small kilt. And it was probably invented by an Englishman. In 1727 the chief of the Glengarry MacDonnells leased his ancient hardwood forests of Invergarry to Thomas Rowlandson, an English ironmaster from Barrow in Lancashire. Part of the deal obliged Glengarry to supply workers from among his clansmen to cut the forests and stoke the furnaces. Rowlandson noticed how the *feile mor*, the big kilt, hampered men and that near the furnaces and falling trees loose garments could be dangerous.

Until 1727 the big kilt had simply been a large plaid, a piece of rough checked-weave material, usually about five feet across and fifteen feet long, more like tweed than the smooth modern tartan. *Plaide* is the Gaelic word for a blanket, and it was used as day wear and for sleeping under. To put it on a clansman laid the plaid on the ground over his belt and then lay down himself. He then wrapped the bottom section around his waist and secured it by buckling his belt and arranging the excess material in pleats at the back. The rest covered the upper body like a loose coat and it was usually pinned at the shoulder. A Roman toga worked on similar principles.

Rowlandson could see that the big kilt would hinder production, and so he contacted the garrison tailor at Inverness. A design came back for a shorter kilt, half the size, belted at the waist, pleated at the back but with no covering of the upper body. It became known as the *feile beag*, the small kilt, and was soon adopted as a standard style by the army and by non-Highlanders.

To add cultural insult to cultural injury, the word *kilt* is also English. It was originally used as a verb in Middle English (and still is in modern English) to mean the business of hitching up a skirt and tucking it in at the waist or in undergarments.

To make matters even worse, tartan is not a Gaelic or a Scottish or an English word. It almost certainly comes from *tiretaine*, an Old French term for heavy material of no particular colour. It was in currency hundreds of years ago and was first written down in 1538 and a specific association immediately made as *Heland tartane*. And by the 16th century it appears that yarn was being dyed and woven into colourful checked patterns. The palette available from plants in the Highlands is wide and extracts can be very bright and eye-catching. For example, a rich dark green can be found in the stems of bluebells and a matt black from their roots. Blaeberries make a purple dye, bog myrtle gives yellow and tormentil a vivid red.

Dyes could run easily if not properly fixed, but the means of doing this in a pre-industrial society was surprising. Instead of chemicals like alum, human urine was the favoured fixative. Known in Gaelic as *mun*, it was carefully collected in Highland households, then allowed to mature before being passed on to spinners and weavers.

While lords in small, dye-fast kilts and ladies in tartan sashes managed not to fall over their feet in the pas de bas at Queen Victoria's Highland balls, and reeled their way into royal favour, revolution was at last stirring in the Highland glens and straths. As clan society disintegrated and the emigration ships sailed those who remained found themselves rent-paying tenants of a set of mostly absent landlords, some of them English. Many farmers had been forced off their ancient territories down to the rocky coasts where they had been allocated *lots* or what became known as *crofts*. These were in essence smallholdings, although they could vary in size depending on the geography and the quality of the ground. The potato helped sustain life and fishing could provide a much needed source of protein. But it was no more than a subsistence economy – and a fragile one. Crofters had few rights. They could be summarily evicted and, if the rents were more than nominal, arrears could trigger removal very quickly. By the second half of the 19th century trouble was brewing.

Near Portree, on the Isle of Skye, the crofters of the district of Braes had long depended on the communal grazings on Ben Lee. When Lord MacDonald, the chief of the name and a wide landowner on Skye, sold Ben Lee to a sheep farmer, the families of Braes found themselves in grave difficulties, with nowhere to graze their animals. When a petition to Lord

OPPOSITE *Highland dancing attracted competitors of different ages and varying levels of confidence in the early 20th century.*

ABOVE *The Reel of Tulloch is danced in the heather for a 19th-century photograph of the picturesque school.*

OPPOSITE *The interior of a weaver's cottage on Islay, 1772.*

MacDonald was rejected the crofters began a rent strike, refusing to pay. On 7 April 1882 a Sheriff-Officer attempted to serve eviction notices in Braes. They were burned in front of him. A battle followed.

When warrants to arrest five of the Braes crofters were issued, the Sheriff of Inverness-shire realized that a substantial force of policemen would be needed. Fifty constables from Glasgow arrived in Skye by steamer and they marched immediately to Braes. It was raining steadily and Sheriff Ivory (who travelled in a coach) no doubt hoped that tempers would be dampened. He was quickly disappointed.

On a narrow stretch of the road from Portree to Braes, where there is a sea-cliff on one side and the steeply rising slopes of Ben Lee on the other, the constables and their Sheriff were ambushed. A furious fight followed. Stones rained down on the police, and they in turn drew their truncheons and repeatedly charged into the crowd of men, women and children. There was blood on the grass as the crofter families tried desperately to free the five

men who had been arrested, and it took an all-out last charge for the constables and Sheriff Ivory to break out and flee back to Portree.

The Battle of the Braes was widely reported. A year later the Highland
Land League was formed to co-ordinate resistance and demand reform.
There were land raids on Lewis and elsewhere in the Highlands unrest continued to flare. Significantly the motto of the Highland Land League harked
back to the time of the clans, to the ideas wrapped up in the word *dùthchas*.
It was 'Is Treasa Tuath na Tighearna', and it means the Kindred is mightier
than the Lord. A simple summary of the complex traditions that produced
the anger and determination behind the motto was made 80 years before,
when the Countess of Sutherland began evicting her tenants in the north-
eastern Highlands:

> *They argued that they had a prescriptive claim to the soil: that they did*
> *their lady justice if they farmed it as their fathers had done; and that,*

Les Montagnards d'Ecosse en
leur habits accûtumés avec
un manteau pendant.

Berg-Schotten in gewöhn
Aufzug mit herab hang
der Decke.

Un Montagnard d'Ecosse qui prend son
manteau sur les épaules, quâd il va pleuvoir.
Ein seine Decke gagé der Regē, gleich
eine Mantel über die Schul-
ter a schlagender Berg-
Schott.

Johan Christian Leopold excudit Augu.

ABOVE *An 18th-century French engraving showing how the belted plaid could be worn.*
OPPOSITE *Highland couple in the late 19th century.*

> *chieftainess though she were, she had no better title to eject them from their*
> *humble tenements than they had to drive her from her castle.*

W. E. Gladstone was Prime Minister in the 1880s and he found himself
under pressure in the House of Commons from a newly elected group
of Highland Land League MPs. The Napier Commission was convened
to investigate, and the Crofters Act of 1886 guaranteed tenure and
allowed crofts to be passed on from one generation to the next without
interference. It was the first victory for ordinary Highlanders for a very
long time.

The Highland Land League had been founded in London and the role of
expatriates began to have an influence. Clan societies formed. First was Clan
MacNaughton in 1878, followed by Clan MacKay in 1888. By 1900 there
were scores and one Glasgow newspaper sniffed:

> *[there are] innumerable Highland clan societies that are swaggering in tartan,*
> *painfully acquiring the pronunciation of their respective battle-cries, and*
> *searching for chiefs.*

It was an unfair observation. In addition to adding greatly to the store of
historical material on individual clans, the societies have at least re-created

some sense of a collective identity out of the wide diaspora. In modern times the internet has been an effective means of recruitment and regular contact for those dispersed to the corners of the earth by the Clearances.

For the summer of 2009 a huge clan gathering was planned for the Queen's Park in Edinburgh. Below the red sandstone of Salisbury Crags more than a hundred clan pavilions were to be set up, a vast music stage built and countless marquees raised around an arena where hammers would be thrown and cabers tossed. For months beforehand disaster was predicted: no one would come, it was too expensive and the clan pavilions would be the resort only of a few pathetic enthusiasts. But in two days of glowing July sunshine sixty thousand appeared, as if from nowhere. No one expected the throngs of North Americans, Australians and English expatriates, many of them kilted and tartaned, all of them delighted to be with people of the same name. For a sunlit moment clanship was reborn.

9

THE BLOOD IS STRONG

WHEN DR SAMUEL JOHNSON AND HIS COMPANION, JAMES BOSWELL, VISITED THE ISLE OF SKYE IN 1773 THEY WITNESSED SOMETHING DISCONCERTING:

In the evening the company danced as usual. We performed, with much activity, a dance which, I suppose, the emigration from Skye has occasioned. They call it 'America'. Each of the couples, after the common involutions and evolutions, successively whirls round in a circle, till all are in motion; and the dance seems intended to show how emigration catches, till a whole neighbourhood is set afloat.

It was indeed catching, and not only in Skye. Between 1821 and 1915 no less than 44 million people left Europe for the New World, for the USA, Australasia and elsewhere. This enormous and unprecedented shift in population was the principal reason for the rapid development of the USA in particular. The arrival of so many accelerated the movement in the balance of economic power so profoundly that on the eve of the First World War the USA had become dominant.

LEFT *Dr Johnson (1709–84) striding out in the Hebrides.*

OPPOSITE *A lithograph of 1853 by James Fagan entitled* The Emigrants' Farewell.

OVERLEAF *The great international Caledonian games held at Jones Woods, New York City in 1867.*

Two million of these emigrants were Scots and half of them found landfall in the USA. And of these very many were Highlanders. It is reckoned that before 1815 there were more than 30,000 former clansmen and women in the USA, and they took a motive hand in the great events of the last quarter of the 18th century. In 1775 the 13 American colonies rose up in rebellion against the British crown, and events moved quickly.

In the dense pine woods on the western bank of Moore's Creek in North Carolina the glint of claymores could be seen and a whisper of Gaelic made out. Led by Colonel Donald MacLeod, the Cape Fear Highlanders realized that they had not passed unobserved. On the opposite bank of the creek several units of the Continental Army were dug in. From behind an earthen embankment soldiers of the cause of American Independence lay with their muskets at the ready, intently watching the half broken-down bridge across Moore's Creek.

Recruited, sometimes by force, from the recent immigrants from Skye and the Western Highlands, the Cape Fear regiment had rallied around a royal standard. MacLeans, Stewarts, Camerons, MacRaes and many others had mustered at Cross Creek in North Carolina in January 1776 when General Donald MacDonald had raised the standard of George III. It was a remarkable reversal. Men whose clans had fought for the Prince

THE GREAT INTERNA

Held at Jones Woods

This Picture is respectfully dedicated to the S

CALEDONIAN GAMES

ork City July 1st 1867.

e Caledonian Clubs throughout the United States

at Culloden sharpened their broadsword to defend the interests of the Hanoverians. Even more surprisingly, General MacDonald's cousin, Allan MacDonald of Kingsburgh in Skye, also led a contingent of former clansmen to the muster. And with him was his wife, Flora MacDonald, the daring woman who had famously helped Prince Charles escape to France after Culloden. Clearly revolutionary republicanism horrified the conservative Highlanders and their instinct, or more precisely, the instinct of their leaders, was to support the monarchy, any monarchy.

When Colonel Donald MacLeod led the clansmen through the pine trees towards the broken bridge across Moore's Creek he could see that it was still passable. The planking of the roadway had been destroyed, but the wooden piers were still intact. What MacLeod could not know was that the Continental troops on the other side had deliberately left the bridge just usable in order to entice the Highlanders to attempt to cross. Grease, tallow and soap had been smeared on the standing piers, and behind the earthen embankment nearby muskets and artillery were primed and aimed at the bridge.

ABOVE *James Oglethorphe visits the Highland Colony in Georgia that he chartered for unemployed men freed from debtor's prison.*

'King George and Broadswords!' was the agreed cry to signal the launch of an attack, probably shouted in Gaelic, and Donald MacLeod went first. Using the point of his sword to keep his balance on the slippery piers the Colonel somehow reached the other side and in a crazy, impetuous gesture charged alone up the earthen bank into a hail of musket fire. He was probably dead before he fell. Behind him, the Highlanders struggling over the bridge were blown to bits, and many on the far bank fled or surrendered. No Highland charge was made, except the hopeless and courageous attack by Donald MacLeod, and no close quarter fighting was possible. Like Culloden, the Battle of Moore's Bridge was a debacle, a last, little known and ignominious defeat for a way of life. Most of the Cape Fear Highlanders were allowed to return to their farms on condition that they took an oath to put away their broadswords forever.

Chain migration was the mechanism that brought the Skye men and others from the Western Highlands to North Carolina. The pioneers who came first encouraged and gave early shelter and help to their relatives and fellow clansmen who followed. It made for close communities and distinctive enclaves.

Some immigrants arrived in North America as soldiers in the British army. Hugh Fraser fought with the Fraser Highlanders in the St Lawrence Basin and at the Heights of Abraham and in 1763 he brought his wife and brother-in-law to settle in the Mohawk Valley in upstate New York. There a clan chief, or someone who appears to have modelled himself closely

ABOVE *South Australian Scottish Infantry wearing ceremonial dress.*

on one, ruled over a huge swathe of the valley and spent tremendous energy developing his 700,000 acres. Sir William Johnson seemed to attract Highland immigrants and in 1774 a large party of 425 arrived in the Mohawk Valley from Fort William. They were made welcome and in turn grew into a successful and enduring community.

Sometimes emigration happened in stages. In the 1820s the Rev. Norman MacLean led a group from Assynt, in the north west of Scotland, to settle in Canada. But in the 1850s they moved halfway around the world to Waipu in New Zealand. Once established, the Assynt people wrote to those left behind in the Highlands and successive waves of emigration crossed the seas in the 19th and early 20th centuries. Some say that Invercargill near the southern tip of New Zealands's South Island is a more Scottish city than any in Scotland.

In Cape Breton Island, just to the north-east of the Nova Scotia peninsula, Gaelic is still spoken. Immigrants began coming in numbers from 1802 and by the 1850s two thirds of the island's population of 55,000 was thought to have originated from the Highlands. Gaelic was therefore the first language of the majority of new Cape Bretoners and it was widely heard in the streets of towns and villages as recently as the 1930s. Now the Gaelic community has dwindled dramatically, but the memories of old traditions survive. The celebrated Canadian writer and Cape Breton native, Alistair MacLeod, recalled:

BELOW *The first gathering of the Bendigo Caledonian Society in Australia, 1890.*

Scottish settlers in Waipu, New Zealand, who had sailed on migration ships from Nova Scotia in the 1850s, enjoying a reunion in 1903.

My grandmother gets up and goes for her violin which hangs on a peg inside her bedroom door. It is a very old violin and came from the Scotland of her ancestors, from the crumbled foundations that now dot and haunt Lochaber's shores. She plays two Gaelic airs – Gun Bhris Mo Chridh' On Dh'Fhalbh Thu and Cha Till Mi Tuille. Her hands have suffered stiffness and the lonely laments waver and hesitate as do the trembling fingers on the four taut strings. She is very moved by the ancient music and there are tears within her eyes.

Several strands of the musical traditions of the Highlands have survived and even thrived into the modern era. One of them is unique, and closely associated with the particular strain of fundamentalist religion that has gripped parts of the Highlands, and especially the Islands in the last 150 years. Gaelic psalms are sung in the protestant churches of Lewis and elsewhere. The arrangement is unmistakable. The man standing *air ceann na seinn*, at the head of the singing, is known as the precentor. This remarkable form involves him singing a line of the psalm to the congregation, who then return it, hung with grace notes. Swooping and soaring like a flight of birds, stately and powerful, the psalm is sung without music and the effect is stunning. There can be few more beautiful canons of church music, and none that express absolute belief so dramatically.

The Free Church of Scotland, what became known as *The Wee Free*, was established in 1900 when some congregations refused to join the new United Presbyterian Church of Scotland. Further schisms took place in the 20th and 21st centuries, but the overall tone of the free churches is similar. They are fundamentalists, still immensely influential in some Highland communities and stubbornly independent. Sunday observance is important and how their influence manifests itself to most outsiders. The exuberance of the psalms stands in high contrast with the conservatism of the beliefs of the people who sing them.

OPPOSITE *Known as* The Thin Red Line, *the 93rd Sutherland Highlanders at the Battle of Balaclava during the Crimean War in 1854.*

BELOW Scottish Settlers in North America *by Thomas Faed, a 19th-century Scottish artist.*

The Free Church is a well-known Highland institution, more visible than its numbers warrant, but it is declining steadily, its congregations ageing and not renewing themselves. A similar fate awaits the Gaelic language, the repository of so much of the history of the clans. But strenuous efforts are being made to revive it, or at least arrest its decline. Most eye catching is the initiative to found and fund Gaelic playgroups for nursery children, and at the other end of the educational spectrum, a Gaelic-medium college at Sabhal Mòr Ostaig in Skye. And a new television channel began broadcasting in 2008. BBC Alba is working hard to attract non-Gaelic speakers as well as the diminishing community of fluent speakers.

What might save Gaelic, or create better conditions for its salvation, is DNA. In recent times there has been nothing less than an explosion of interest in genealogy, particularly among widely scattered diasporas. From Cape Fear to the suburbs of Glasgow, expatriate Highlanders are tracing back their origins to the time of the clans. And some of the research has turned up fascinating results. Scientists at the University of Edinburgh have discovered that a huge percentage of men with the surname of MacDonald, Donaldson or Donald are descended from a single lineage. It is Norse in origin. There are approximately 1.6 million MacDonalds (and variant surnames) in the world and it appears that a quarter are descended from one man. The progenitor of 400,000 people is very likely to have been Somerled the Viking, the first Lord of the Isles and the founder of Clan Donald. It seems that the blood is still strong.

10

CAMUSDARROCH

HERE IS A ROAD, AN OLD SINGLE-TRACK ROAD BETWEEN ARISAIG AND MORAR THAT THREADS ITS WAY THROUGH THE HISTORY OF THE SCOTTISH HIGHLANDS AND THE CLANS. Mostly without fences or dykes on either side, it brings travellers from Fort William out to the west and the Atlantic shore, first following the north side of Loch Eil and then passing the Glenfinnan Monument at the head of Loch Shiel. The mountains rise steeply as the road winds past Loch Eilt. There are few houses, no settlements and the sense of wilderness stretches far into the distance. No one seems to work the landscape, no shepherd whistles after his dogs, no farmer's tractor pulls a trailer. Only the cars on the road break the silence as they move through the emptiness.

When it meets the ocean at Loch nan Uamh, the story and the road at last take on some colour. Beside the loch stands a cairn marking the place where Prince Charles made landfall in 1745. Almost 2,000 metres above, the great mountain of Sidhean Mor glowers down. Almost immediately the wastes of the mountainside and the sea disappear as the road plunges into a dense oak forest. Hanging woods darken on either side and Gaelic describes the place simply as *Druimindarroch*, the Oak Ridge.

At the fishing village of Arisaig there is a quay snaking into the sea-loch and the clutter of fishing is piled beside a straggle of tin-roofed huts. A post office, a shop and a hotel make the village feel homely. As the road climbs above the houses and breasts a rise, a vast and heart-breakingly beautiful panorama opens. Out in the ocean lie the islands of Skye, Rum, Muck and Eigg, and the breakers roll onshore, washing beaches of brilliant white sand. Immediately inland is a wide swathe of machair, salt-sprayed grassland grazed short and green by a scattering of sheep and cows. Here are farm houses, at Back of Keppoch, Bunacaimb and Portnaluchaig, and the mountains

ABOVE *The Glenfinnan Monument raised where Prince Charles landed in 1745 at the head of Loch Shiel.*

OVERLEAF *Loch Eil and Fort William in the 19th century.*

of South Morar seem to shrink back. Here are the marks of people, of cultivation and stock rearing, of human hands shaping the land.

This is MacDonald country. On the Sleat peninsula to the north-west stands Armadale Castle, once the seat of the clan chiefs, now where the Clan Donald Centre opens its doors to visitors. Due west lies Rum, an island home for almost 500 people – until 1828. In that awful year all of them were cleared off the land and forced onto emigrant ships bound for the USA. Eight thousand sheep and a few shepherds took their place.

The road goes on, following the soft undulations of the land, interrupted occasionally by cattle grids and humped-backed bridges. Two miles south of Morar it passes by its ultimate glory, a place easy to miss, a place of astonishing splendour.

Camusdarroch, the Oak Bay, is best seen in the evening when a summer sun is dying behind the distant Cuillin ridge on Skye. The white sand reflects the last glimmers, heightening what light is left, while out in the ocean the islands shadow into silhouette. Sitting in the high dunes, in the warmth of the

gloaming, senses are heightened too. This beauty, this flower of the west, was seen by a thousand generations, by men and women who lived in or came by this remarkable place. Some were on this shore every day, many others passed it on the old road, some sailed in the bay, fishing, travelling, playing, learning.

They all knew that Camusdarroch was beautiful, glorious, evocative – and home. All over the Highlands and islands there are places like it, places of intimate loveliness, places of majestic grandeur. And it was precisely this beauty that animated the story of the clans, that prompted the poetry, the music, the passion and the countless examples of extraordinary courage. What sped the clansmen into the charge at Culloden were the names of their places and the memory of their great beauty. It was what bound them to the land for millennia, what formed the rhythms of their language, and what tore out their hearts as the white-sailed ships slipped over the horizon.

At Camusdarroch the army of the dead muster once more, the ghosts of an immense past whisper among the waving grass of the sand dunes, they flit between the darkening trees and murmur their memories as a breeze freshens off the ocean and night falls.

BELOW *The westering sun over Arisaig.*

11

THE CLANS

HAT FOLLOWS IS AN ALPHABETICAL LIST OF THE CLANS WHOSE territory was in the Scottish Highlands, and who played an important role in the politics of medieval and early modern Britain. The surnames of the Lowlands, such as the Armstrongs and Elliots, are not included even though they now call themselves clans.

Highland clans have – broadly – five distinct cultural origins. From the north and north-west come the Norse clans such as the MacLeods, the MacSweens, the Gunns, the MacIvors and the MacAulays. Although they were assimilated into a Gaelic-speaking society, many of the place names in the Hebrides remember the Vikings of the 9th to the 13th centuries. Almost all of the place names on the Isle of Lewis, for example, are Norse.

The enigmatic Pictish kingdoms of the Dark Ages disappeared, but their people did not, and most of the clans of the eastern and central Highlands are descended from them. Clan Chattan is only the most famous, and obvious.

In the west the MacDonalds are the most numerous representatives of the Dalriadic clans, those with the strongest links to Ireland. They were always Gaelic speaking and acquired a royal lustre with the Lordship of the Isles, a largely MacDonald enterprise. Their neighbours, Clan Campbell and their satellites, probably had their beginnings as kindreds in the Old Welsh-speaking kingdoms of Strathclyde and Manau. They seemed often to be a group apart. Perhaps the most surprising are those Anglo-Norman families who came north, often from the Borders and usually at the prompting of King David in the first half of the 12th century. The Frasers, the Grants, the Stewarts, the Menzies, the Chisholms and others are now so completely identified with the Highlands that the French origins of their names are forgotten.

Where the clan is known by a Mac name the second element has in all cases been capitalized in order to show its origins more clearly and the Mac is always rendered as Mac rather than Mc. Some names, such as Mackenzie and Mackintosh, have only one capital and sometimes begin with Mc. No offence is intended.

BEATON

Hereditary physicians to the MacDonald Lords of the Isles, this family became doctors to the Stewart kings, Charles II being the last to be treated by a Beaton.

BLAIR

From a Gaelic word for field or battlefield, the name is found in Perthshire and other parts of Scotland and it dates back to the 12th century.

BRODIE

An ancient family that originated in the Moray coastlands, around the town of Forres. The name of the town is thought to derive from the tribe of the Boresti and the Brodies themselves may have Pictish beginnings.

BRUCE

The name of the Scottish royal family after the early 14th century; it is Norman-French in origin, the de Brus probably coming from the Cotentin peninsula.

BUCHAN

Also the name of the district of north-east Scotland at the easternmost tip of the Moray Firth, Buchan came to be a clan name and was associated with the Hays, Keiths, Frasers and Comyns.

BUCHANAN

The clan lands were on the fringes of the Highlands, on the southern banks of Loch Lomond. Clarinch, a small island in the loch, is their battle cry. The line of chiefs fell extinct in 1762, but an emigrant, James Buchanan, became the 15th president of the United States.

BURNETT

Another clan with Norman-French origins, the Burnetts had their seat in the beautiful castle of Crathes in Aberdeenshire.

CAMERON

Born some time around 1400, Black Donald brought together the confederacy of kindreds which became Clan Cameron and established their territory in Lochaber. A long line of great and charismatic chiefs followed, many given the Christian name of Ewan and all attached to the district of Loch Eil. When Prince Charles landed in 1745 his charm was said to have overcome Cameron of Locheil's better judgment and what was known as the fiercest, most warlike clan made the rebellion possible. The forfeited lands of Lochaber were later restored and Camerons continued to be active in politics as MPs and soldiers. The 24th chief, who died in 1905, was MP for Invernessshire and sat on the Crofters' Commission chaired by Lord Napier. The Cameron Highlanders were raised in 1793 and later amalgamated with the Seaforth Highlanders to form the Queen's Own Highlanders. The present chief occupies the mansion house at Achnacarry. The name of Cameron probably derives from the Gaelic nickname of *cam-shron*. It means Bent or Broken Nose, a good name for a warlike clan.

CAMPBELL

Based on a Gaelic nickname *cam-beul*, which means twisted mouth, Clan Campbell probably originated among the Old Welsh-speaking kindreds of the ancient kingdom of Strathclyde. If they did not speak Gaelic, their mouths or speech were twisted. Campbell lands began to expand from a nucleus around Loch Awe and eventually occupied much of Argyll and the south-western Highlands. Campbell support for government authority did not always guarantee favour. Two Earls of Argyll were executed for treason in the dynastic upheavals of the 17th century, but by 1701 William III had elevated the chiefs to the rank of dukes. By the time of the rebellion of 1745, which they did not support, the Campbells were by far the most powerful clan in Scotland. The Duke of Argyll's principal seat is Inveraray Castle, close by their planned town of Inveraray on the shores of Loch Fyne.

CARMICHAEL

The first element of the name is likely to be *caer*, Old Welsh for a fort, which suggests southern origins but some Carmichaels moved into the western Highlands and became kinsmen of the Appin Stewarts.

CLAN CHATTAN

This federation of clans has a long, unique and fascinating history. The name literally means the Clan of the Cats, more precisely the Wildcats, perhaps a reference to the now extinct Scottish lynx or bobcat. Their motto is 'Touch not the Catt [but] with a glove'. An ancient name, Caithness means Cat-Cape, *Cataibh* is the

Gaelic name for Sutherland and *Machair Chat* and *Braigh Chat* are old names for parts of the county. Gaels call the Duke of Sutherland *Morair Chat* or sometimes *Diuc Chat* and those who live in Sutherland are *Catach*. Clan Chattan first comes on record in the 14th century, but appears to grow quickly into an alliance of MacPhersons, Cattanachs, MacBeans or MacBains, MacPhails, Shaws, Farquharsons, Ritchies, MacCombies, MacThomases, MacGillivrays, Davidsons and others. From an early date the chiefs of Clan Chattan seem always to have been Mackintoshes. They were titled as Captains of Clan Chattan until 1947 when they were finally recognized formally as chiefs. Their arms show a wildcat rampant and one of their most famous sons in modern times remembered all those feline associations. When Charles Rennie Mackintosh designed his first interior in Glasgow (his own flat) it was decorated with a frieze of cats.

CHISHOLM

Originating from the Borders, and another Anglo-Norman clan, the Chisholms moved to the banks of Loch Ness when Robert Chisholm became royal constable of Castle Urquhart. The name of these incomers supplied Gaelic speakers with an awkward pronunciation, and the clan is known as *Siosal* (pron. Showshall) or *na Siosalach*. The Chisholm regiment fought bravely at Culloden and lost their captain, Roderick, a younger son of the chief. The name is still common in the Borders.

COLQUHOUN

Neighbours of the Buchanans on Loch Lomondside, they were badly beaten by the MacGregors in one of the bloodiest battles of the Age of the Forays, in 1602 at Glenfruin. Colquhoun chiefs were governors of the mighty castle on Dumbarton Rock, ancient Alt Clut, the Rock of the Clyde. Dumbarton comes from its Gaelic name of *Dun Breatainn*, but it is unlikely that the Colquhouns were originally an Old Welsh speaking kindred. Awkward to pronunce: if the lq and h are omitted, the name sounds like Cahoon.

COMYN OR CUMMING

An enormously powerful Norman-French family in medieval Scotland, they held lands in the south and the Highlands. The Comyns were rivals of the Bruces and suffered after Robert the Bruce's victory at Bannockburn in 1314.

DAVIDSON

Part of the Clan Chattan confederacy, the Davidsons held land in Badenoch and were kinsmen to the notorious Alexander Stewart, the Wolf of Badenoch.

DONALD OR DONALDSON

These are variants on the name of MacDonald and their history should be seen as part of the story of the Lordship of the Isles.

DRUMMOND

Like many of the more successful clans of the late medieval period, the Drummonds chose the winning side in the Wars of Independence. At the Battle of Bannockburn Sir Malcolm de Drymen or Drummond strewed the ground with deadly caltrops, spiked balls which inflicted ugly injuries on the feet of the heavy horses of the English cavalry. Drummond chiefs were unfailing Stuart supporters and James VII elevated James Drummond to be the first Duke of Perth. Exile after 1746 meant that lands and titles were forfeit, and only restored in 1853 when George Drummond was installed by Act of Parliament as Earl of Perth. War-making and rebellion were banished to history and replaced by peace-making when the 18th Earl of Perth and Chief of Clan Drummond became the first Secretary General of the League of Nations.

ERSKINE

The Erskines were from the southern fringes of the Highlands and became Earls of Mar, an ancient Pictish lordship. After 'Bobbing' John Erskine's leadership of the 1715 rebellion it took many generations for their titles to be restored. The chiefs of the clan are now Earls of Mar and Kellie (in Fife). The fluctuations of Erskine fortunes are a good example of how often and how far clan territories move and how difficult it is to separate the rise and fall of their chiefs from the fate of their people. Originally their lands were at Erskine, near Renfrew on the Clyde; the chiefs later acquired large tracts of the eastern Highlands in Aberdeenshire and became active Jacobites, and then acquired land in Fife. The Erskines may not qualify as a clan on strict definitions, but the political activities of their chiefs insist a place be found.

FARQUHARSON

Neighbours to the Erskines on the Braes of Mar in Upper Deeside, the allegiance of the Farquharsons was never in doubt as the clan turned out for the Stuart cause again and again. Colonel Anne, who raised Clan Mackintosh for the Prince in defiance of her husband, was first Anne Farquharson, daughter of the chief of the name and someone who understood the old bonds of the Clan Chattan federation. She and her relatives formed part of an alternative aristocracy as her brother, James, married Amelia, daughter of Lord George Murray. When James died in 1815 his daughter, Catherine, carried on the tradition of strong Farquharson women when she was recognized as chief. In 1941 Myrtle Farquharson of Invercauld, the then chief, was tragically killed in an air raid.

ABOVE *Men of the Lovat Scouts who served in the Boer War at the beginning of the 20th century.*

FERGUSSON

Committed Jacobites, the Fergussons came out in 1715 and 1745. The name has been anglicized. MacFergus or more correctly, MacFhearghuis, could be an alternative.

FORBES

Clan Forbes has a wonderful origin legend. Their territory between the Grampians and the Moray coast in Banff and Buchan once belonged to a bear. Savage and terrible, it rendered the countryside uninhabitable, until it was killed by Ochonochar, the first chief of Clan Forbes. They feuded often with their neighbours, the Gordons, and this plunged the chiefs deeper and deeper into debt, obliging them to sell land. Unusually the Forbes still live in the same place. Ranked as the premier barons of Scotland, the chiefs live at Balforbes on the River Don.

FRASER

An Anglo-Norman clan whose name probably derives from the lordship of Frezelière in Anjou, they fought alongside Robert the Bruce at the Battle of Bannockburn. One branch of the family settled in Buchan and converted the fishing village of Faithlie into the town of Fraserburgh. The Lovat Frasers flourished around Beauly and fought in the 1745 rebellion. Their chiefs were often called Simon and an alternative Gaelic name for the clan is MacShimi, the sons of Simon. Simon Fraser, Lord Lovat, was beheaded on Tower Hill in London for treason on 9 April 1747. In 1899 Lord Lovat raised the Lovat Scouts, who fought with distinction in the Boer War and both world wars.

GALBRAITH

Based in Stirlingshire, the first recorded chief of the name was Gilchrist Bretnach who flourished at the end of the 12th century. Bretnach means British, or a speaker of Old Welsh, and not Gaelic.

GORDON

An Old Welsh name, meaning strong fort, originally from a village in Berwickshire, it was applied to an Anglo-Norman family who came to the north-east in the 14th century. The Gordons became Earls of Huntly and, for a while, Dukes of Gordon. The family supported both sides in the Jacobite rebellions and were probably the most powerful clan in the north-east. Their motto and their history seem linked: *bydand* is a Scots word meaning durable or stubborn. George Gordon was perhaps the clan's most illustrious son. As Lord Byron, he was a poet who lived an epic, heroic life, dying for the cause of Greek Independence in 1824.

GRANT

With wide territories in Strathspey, Glen Moriston and Glen Urquhart, the Grants were originally an Anglo-Norman clan, the name probably deriving from le Grand. Their lands were important to them and an entertaining but apocryphal story has the chief refusing a peerage from James VI and I with 'And wha'll be the Laird o' Grant?' Most of the clan remained Hanoverian in the rebellions and were not therefore subject to persecution. As landholders in Strathspey, the Grants lent their name and clan motto to a famous brand of whisky known as Grant's Standfast.

GUNN

One of the few Norse clans with a clear ancestral history, they come from Gunni, a Norse Orcadian whose wife inherited great estates in Caithness and Sutherland.

They are thought to be descended from Olaf, King of Man and the Hebrides. War-like and restless, the Gunns often fought with their neighbours, the MacKays and Clan Keith, but they were Hanoverian in 1745. Like the Gordons, they count a great writer among their modern sons. Neil Gunn wrote memorably about the ancient clan lands in *Highland River* (1937).

HAY

Holding lands in Perthshire, they were a Norman-French family who were ardent Jacobites and their clansmen followed the Stewart standard in 1715 and 1745.

HENDERSON

A community with the name Maceanruig lived in Glencoe and translated their name as Henderson, Eanruig being Gaelic for Henry. They took the role of bodyguards to the chiefs of the Glencoe MacDonalds.

INNES

An anglicized version of Aonghas, or Angus, this family settled in the Moray coastlands and, although Covenanters, they supported Charles II in 1650.

KEITH

An ancient Moray family, the Keiths supported Charles II and later Prince Charles Edward Stuart. They forfeited their lands and became soldiers and politicians in Europe.

LAMONT

The Lamonts are probably descended from the Ui Neill, a powerful Irish family based in Ulster. The name is derived from the Gaelic *ladhman*, which means lawman or law-giver. Chiefs of the Lamonts come on record very early, in the 13th century; they held lands in the Cowal peninsula on the Clyde. They suffered from being neighbours of the Campbells. When Sir James Lamont supported the royalist cause in 1643 his territory was invaded by a large Campbell army. When they laid siege to his castles at Toward and Ascog Sir James agreed to surrender them on condition his people were spared. To their lasting shame the Campbells reneged, threw Sir James into prison at Dunstaffnage and slaughtered 200 Lamont clansmen. Despite some redress when the Earl of Argyll was executed for treason in 1661, the Lamonts never recovered. By 1893 the last of the clan lands had been sold and the chiefs emigrated to Australia, where the line still carries on.

LECKIE

Possibly an Old Welsh-speaking family, the Leckies had their origins in Stirlingshire and were connected to Clan Gregor.

LINDSAY

The family came to Scotland in the early 12th century with King David I and may have been natives of Lincolnshire. Ludovic Lindsay fought alongside Montrose at Philiphaugh in 1645 and was captured.

LIVINGSTONE

Having settled in northern Perthshire, around Callendar, the Livingstones came out for the Stewarts in 1715 and forfeited their lands.

MACALISTER

With various spellings, this clan name came from Alasdair Mor MacDonald, the great-grandson of Somerled, Lord of the Isles. Also using the surname of Alexander, the family held land near Stirling.

MACALLAN

Related to Clan Grant, this family was native to Speyside and the Moray area. They gave their name to one of Scotland's greatest malt whiskies.

MACALPINE

Although this was the name of the king from whom all Scottish kings are numbered, Kenneth MacAlpine, the clan name has had an obscure history. The clan is landless and currently has no chief.

MACARTHUR

With territory in Argyll and close links with the Campbells, the MacArthurs were probably of Old Welsh descent. They fought on both sides in the Jacobite rebellions and after Culloden they emigrated in large numbers. John MacArthur introduced the merino sheep to Australia in the early 19th century and is said to have planted the first vineyard there. Arthur MacArthur was a Lieutenant-General in the Union Army in the American Civil War and his son, Douglas, commanded US forces in the Pacific during the Second World War.

OVERLEAF *The Scottish crown jewels emerge during the visit of George IV to Edinburgh in 1822 and are, surprisingly, guarded by Clan Gregor.*

MacAskill

With strong Hebridean connections, this Norse clan has a direct Scandinavian equivalent. Deriving from a Gaelic rendition of son of Asgeir, it also appears across the North Sea as Asgeirsson.

MacAulay

Two distinct branches of this name exist. In the south the MacAulays were closely associated with the MacGregors and held lands from the Earls of Lennox. By 1767 the last chief of the MacAulays had sold the clan lands to the Campbells. The MacAulays of Lewis believe that they were simply the sons of Olaf, a Norse warlord. One of their chiefs was known as Domhnall Camm, Donald the One-Eyed. He fought alongside Montrose and Alasdair MacColla in their great campaign, but was killed at the Battle of Auldearn. One of Donald Camm's descendants was the 19th-century historian Thomas Babington MacAulay, best known for his *History of England* and the *Lays of Ancient Rome* (1834–38). He made little of his Highland ancestry, even though he was MP for Edinburgh for several years.

MacBain

Part of the Clan Chattan confederacy, the clan traces its line from a name-father, Macbain, in the late 13th century in Moray. The heroic Gillies MacBain, who died at Culloden, was said to be a giant at 6 foot, 4 inches, and he was one of the last of the line of chiefs.

MacBeth

The only patronymic to be found in the line of Scottish kings, MacBeth was also the name-father of the clan and King of Moray before he defeated and killed King Duncan in 1040.

MacCaig

Associated with both Clan MacLeod and Clan Mackenzie, the MacCaig lands were in the north-west, the sphere of influence of both of the larger clans. One of Scotland's very greatest poets, Norman MacCaig (1910–96), drew inspiration from his annual visits to Assynt, a district of the mainland opposite the island of Lewis.

MacCallum

'Maol' is a Gaelic word for shavenhead, or monk, and the first element of the names of MacCallums or Malcolms recalls that. The second part is from

Columba, the great Irish saint who established Iona, and so the clan was first known as the Servants of Columba.

MacColl

Probably a branch of Clan Donald, the MacColls occupied lands around Loch Fyne. In 1602 many of their clansmen were slaughtered in a battle with Clan MacPherson.

MacCrimmon

Probably a Norse clan, the MacCrimmons were based on Skye and were famous as pipers to the chiefs of Clan MacLeod and also ardent supporters of the Hanoverian kings. When Donald Ban MacCrimmon was held captive by Jacobite forces in 1745 their pipers refused to play while the greatest of them all languished in prison.

MacDiarmid

Closely associated with Clan Campbell and holding lands in Glenlyon, the MacDiarmids had a martial reputation and clansmen bearing the name were found in the Atholl regiment in the early 18th century.

MacDonald

A large clan with several branches, each of which merits individual treatment, Clan Donald was a mighty influence in the medieval period through the Lordship of the Isles, and later as a counterweight to Clan Campbell. The first Donald was the grandson of Somerled the Viking and was master of Kintyre and Islay by 1207. His line reunited the principality. Angus Og MacDonald fought alongside Robert the Bruce at Bannockburn and was handsomely rewarded; his son, John of Islay, was the first formally to resume the title of Lord of the Isles. The advance of Clan Donald was decisively checked at the Battle of Harlaw in 1411. Near Inverurie, it was a bloody encounter (known as Red Harlaw) between the Islesmen and the men of the north-east, under the command of the Earl of Mar. The issue was the succession to the great earldom of Ross. Militarily it was not decisive, but since his losses were so great, Donald, Lord of the Isles, withdrew and could no longer pursue territorial claims in the Lowlands. After the fall of the Lordship in the mid-16th century the branches of Clan Donald began to act separately, but usually came together to go into battle, as at Culloden. The High Chief of the MacDonald is Godfrey, Lord MacDonald, and he now runs a hotel on Skye with his wife.

MACDONALD OF CLAN RANALD

Although he was the eldest son of John of Islay, Ranald did not become Lord of the Isles in the mid-14th century. In what seemed to be an amicable arrangement his younger brother, Donald, took the title. Instead Ranald married the wealthy heiress, Amie MacRuari, and became master of the lands of Garmoran (Moidart and parts of the mainland to the north and south). John of Moidart, the victor on the Field of the Shirts at Loch Lochy, was his descendant and Chief of Clan Ranald. Unhesitating supporters of the Stuarts, the clan nevertheless survived and the line of chiefs, or captains, has endured into modern times.

MACDONALD OF SLEAT

Sleat is the southernmost peninsula of Skye, known in Gaelic as *An t'Eilean Sgitheanach*, or the Winged Island and the location of the Clan Donald Centre. Donald Gorm, Chief of the MacDonalds of Sleat, was proclaimed Chief of all Clan Donald in 1518 and had ambitions to re-create the Lordship of the Isles after the fall of John of Islay in 1493. With his fleet of birlinns he attacked the spectacular Mackenzie castle of Eilean Donan in Loch Duich, but was repulsed. Donald took an arrow in the leg and died from the loss of blood. The clan fought for the Stuarts, but in the 1745 rebellion stayed at home. The Sleat estates were therefore left untouched, although there is now very little MacDonald land left on Skye.

MORE MACDONALDS

Branches of Clan Donald were also identified beyond the main territories. There were MacDonalds of Boisdale, Ardnamurchan, Glenaladale, Kingsburgh, Lochmaddy and Staffa.

MACDONELL OF GLENGARRY

Glengarry is a slight variant on the surname of MacDonald (and often called MacDonald in the historical record); the clan played a prominent role as unfailing Stuart supporters. Perhaps their most colourful chief was Colonel Alasdair Ranaldson MacDonell of Glengarry. The model for Sir Walter Scott's haughty Highland chief, Fergus McIvor, in his novel Waverley, he appears to have made a nuisance of himself in Edinburgh during the visit of George IV in 1822. Much to Scott's irritation, he turned up uninvited in flamboyant tartan costume at several parties. Declaring himself to be the Glengarry, identifying himself by his lands rather than the name of his clan as chiefs were apparently wont to do, he also formed The Society of True Highlanders in opposition to The Celtic Society of Edinburgh. Meanwhile many of his clansmen were forced off the land by high rents and threats of eviction. The Glengarry seems to have been little more than a parody of his clan's distinguished heritage.

MacDougall

Descended in a clear line from Dougall, the eldest son of Somerled, the MacDougalls were powerful. After 1164 they held lands in Argyll, Lorne, Mull, Kerrera, Lismore, Coll and Tiree, and their masons built a string of sea castles to guard their dominions. The imposing ruins at Dunstaffnage and Dunollie are the most famous. But in the early 14th century the MacDougall chiefs found themselves opposing Robert the Bruce. By marriage they were allies of the Comyn family, and when Bruce murdered John Comyn in Dumfries conflict was inevitable. In 1308 Bruce fought the MacDougalls in a vicious battle at the Pass of Brander and, with their defeat, their estates were forfeit. The Campbells were significant beneficiaries and although in time the chiefs retrieved some of their possessions, they never ruled over the islands again.

MacDowall

Gaelic speakers from Ireland settled in Galloway in the 7th and 8th centuries and formed clans. The MacDowalls were one of the most powerful.

MacDuff

The clan claims descent from Gruoch, MacBeth's queen, and with lands in Banffshire and in Fife, the chiefs became great magnates. They had the right to enthrone Scottish kings at their coronation.

MacEwan

Settled around Loch Fyne, the clan has a name-father in the early 12th century. By 1602 they were listed as a broken clan, living outside the law, and the Campbells were made responsible for their good behaviour. They failed.

MacFarlane

With lands at the north end of Loch Lomond Clan MacFarlane took an unusually active part in the politics of Lowland Scotland. Descended from Parlan or Parlane (the p became a ph or f with aspiration), the MacFarlanes fought at Flodden in 1513 and in the first phase of the battle the Highlanders charged and knocked down an English battalion. But as that awful day turned against Scotland, the chief and many of his men were killed. At the Battle of Pinkie in 1547, when Henry VIII was attempting to force the Scots into a dynastic union with the Tudors, the Chief of the MacFarlanes was the royal standard bearer and, again in defeat, he was killed, as were 200 of his clansmen, although 'they were well armed in shirts of mail'. Perhaps chastened by their losses, the MacFarlanes took no part in the 18th-century Jacobite rebellions and their chief, Walter MacFarlane, lived quietly in Edinburgh, a noted antiquary and scholar. By 1767 the remaining clan lands at Arrochar had been sold off and the chief emigrated to North America.

MacFie

The clan were hereditary record keepers for the Lords of the Isles and they held the island of Colonsay. Led by Cameron of Locheil, many MacFies fought at Culloden and after the battle Ewan MacFie became a notorious outlaw.

MacGillivray

Part of Clan Chattan, the clan suffered tremendous casualties at Culloden, and many emigrated to North America soon after. The last chief of the MacGillivrays is believed to have died in Canada.

MacGregor

The clan motto is unequivocal: *'S Rioghal mo Dhream*. Translated as my race is royal, it is a reference to the tradition of Clan Gregor as *Siol Alpin*, the descendants of King Alpin, father of Kenneth MacAlpin. But royalty was almost their nemesis when James VI and I had the name 'altogidder abolished' in 1603 and 170 years of persecution followed. When the ban was lifted in 1774 a remarkable transformation took place. When the MacGregor chiefs were restored one of them, Sir Evan MacGregor, played a central role in the state visit of George IV to Edinburgh in 1822. MacGregor clansmen guarded the recently rediscovered Scottish crown regalia and Sir Evan proposed the toast to 'the chief of chiefs' at a royal banquet. Rob Roy MacGregor would have choked on the wine and pinched the regalia.

MacInnes

The name is from the Gaelic for son of Angus, and they are one of the most ancient names. One of the early kindreds of Dalriada was the Cenel nAonghusa and their descendants appear to have settled in the lands of Morvern. They were skilled archers and the clan crest is an arm and hand holding a bow.

MacIntyre

Sometimes clans were named after jobs, and MacIntyre is from *Mac an t' Saor*, the son of the carpenter. Or more precisely, a shipwright, and the birlinns of the Lords of the Isles were likely first built by MacIntyres.

MacIver

Despite being a Norse clan, the MacIvers had connections in the southern Highlands, especially with Clan Campbell. They were keepers of Inveraray Castle in the late 16th century.

MacKay

In its Gaelic rendering of *MacAoidh*, the origins of the clan might be clearer. It looks as though the Mackays were linked to the extended royal family of Celtic Scotland and Aodh, Abbot of Dunkeld. The Macbeth line and its heirs were cleared from the lands of the south coast of the Moray Firth by David I (and replaced by many who founded clans) and fetched up further north. Certainly by the 14th century they were established in the north-west corner of Scotland, with their principal possessions in Strathnaver. In the 15th century the power of the clan was at its zenith and an army of 4,000 MacKays could be put in the field by their chiefs. But pressure came from their equally powerful neighbours, the Earls of Sutherland. By the beginning of the 17th century the men of Clan Mackay had become a regiment for hire and they found work in Europe in the Thirty Years War. Aeneas MacKay was Brigadier-General of MacKay's Scotch Regiment in the service of the States General of Holland and the family settled in Holland. Honours followed. In 1822, while the clans cheered George IV in Edinburgh, Barthold MacKay was created Baron Ophemert of the Netherlands. The clan chiefs were Dutchmen until 1938 when the new chief became a British subject.

Mackenzie

By 1427 the Mackenzies had emerged from the shadow of Clan Donald and were powerful in Kintail, their famous castle at Eilean Donan held for them by the MacRaes. Theirs is an ancient name: MacCoinneach or MacKenneth in Gaelic. It comes from an Old Welsh hero of the north called Cunedda. He led an army to North Wales to expel the Irish invaders, but is now almost entirely forgotten. Pronounced Kunetha, his name meant Good or Great Leader and is the earliest form of Kenneth. Sons of the Great Chief is what the clan name means. Like the Campbells, the Mackenzies profited from the downfall of Clan Donald and extended their reach to the Hebrides, and in the opposite direction, to Cromarty and the North Sea. For their support of the Jacobite cause, the clan chiefs suffered and their estates greatly diminished. But Mackenzies remain as Earls of Cromarty.

MacKinnon

Like Clan Gregor, the MacKinnons claimed descent from the *Siol Alpin*, the royal house that began to rule much of Scotland in the 9th century. The chiefs became

hereditary Abbots of Iona and the last of these held on until 1500. The MacKinnons marched from the Clyde to join Prince Charles in Edinburgh in 1745. During the flight of the prince after Culloden the chief, Iain Og, sent his birlinn to take Charles to Mallaig, outrunning two government warships. The old chief was over 70, but nevertheless spent five hellish years in the rotting prison hulks moored in the Thames off Tilbury. He died in 1756 and his line became extinct in 1808. The new chiefs have a strong tradition of soldiering.

MACKINTOSH

The derivation is a simple one: it comes from *toiseach*, Gaelic for leader. A Mackintosh regiment fought at Preston in 1715 and afterwards many were transported to the Americas.

MACLACHLAN

The Vikings who raided down the Western seaboard were know to Gaels as *Na Lochlannich* and Clan MacLachlan appear to be a rare southern Norse clan. They held land around Loch Fyne in the heart of Campbell country. This did not discourage their chief from supporting Prince Charles in the 1745 rebellion. When the Jacobite army invaded England MacLachlan was sent north to Perth to gather reinforcements. And nor was he discouraged when the army retreated, for he led 300 of his clansmen onto the field at Culloden. It was said that he was riding from the prince to order the army to advance when he was shot out of the saddle by a cannonball. In a rare intervention the Campbell Duke of Argyll interceded to prevent the MacLachlan estates becoming forfeit. In 1942 Marjorie MacLachlan became 24th chief of the name.

MACLAREN

The clan are said to descend from the Dalriadic kindreds, but more likely come from a 13th-century name-father, Laurence, Abbot of Achtow in Perthshire. In the clan heartland of Balquhidder stands the Boar's Rock, the Creag an Tuirc, the muster point from which the clan war cry is derived. It was last heard when the Appin regiment charged at Culloden.

MACLEAN

Both the MacLeans and the related clan of MacLaine of Lochbuie claim descent from the kings of Dalriada, and a more recent ancestor known as *Gilleathan na Tuaidh*, or Gillean of the Battle Axe. This famous warrior fought against the Norse at the Battle of Largs in 1263. His descendants were given land on Mull by the Lords of the Isles in the 1350s and they built the spectacular sea castle at Duart. John Mor

MacLaine of Lochbuie was a great swordsman and when an Italian fencing master at the court of James V challenged any of the Scottish noblemen to a duel Big John killed him. The MacLeans of Duart, like the Campbells in the south, were usually enemies of the MacDonalds and until they were overcome by debt, kept their independence. Sir Fitzroy MacLean kept up the martial traditions of his clan with heroic action in the former Yugoslavia and an excellent account of his travels in Russia in *Eastern Approaches* (1949).

MacLennan

Covenanters and supporters of the Mackenzie Earl of Seaforth, the MacLennans fought at Auldearn against Montrose and Alasdair MacColla. Led by their great chief, Ruaridh, the clan fought to the death before being cut to pieces by Gordon cavalry. They never recovered their power.

MacLeod

Leod was thought to be the son of the last Norse King of Man and the Northern Hebrides, Olaf the Black. Two branches of the clan established themselves from

PRECEDING PAGES *Kismuil Castle off the Isle of Barra.*
BELOW *Castle Urquhart on the shores of Loch Ness.*

earliest times: the MacLeods of Harris and the MacLeods of Lewis. Dunvegan Castle on the Isle of Skye was also a possession and the seat of the MacLeods of Harris. One of the MacLeod chiefs, Ruaridh Mor, had a famous lament composed for him by his hereditary piper Patrick Mor MacCrimmon. The chiefs took no part in the 1745 rebellion, but groups of MacLeod clansmen stood in the ranks at Culloden.

MacMillan

The origin of the name of the MacMillans is unusual and strongly suggests native Celtic origins for the clan. Gillie Chriosd, the son of Cormac, Bishop of Dunkeld, is commonly held to be the progenitor of the MacMillans. The Celtic monastic tonsure was not like the Roman version, with the crown of the head shaved so that the circle of remaining hair resembled the crown of thorns, the *ceudgelt* was cut across the crown of the head, from ear to ear with the front part shaved to the forehead, and the hair left to grow long down the back. It is thought to have been the Druidic style of pre-Christian Britain. The Celtic version was known as the tonsure of St John, and those who wore it as *Maoil-Iain*, the servants of St John. And so Gillie Chriosd was the son of Cormac, a servant of St John – hence Mac Maoil-Iain or MacMillan. Names tell stories. The clan held lands in Knapdale and the most famous servant of St John was Harold MacMillan, Prime Minister of Great Britain in the late 1950s and early 1960s.

MacNab

Derived from the Gaelic, *Mac an Aba*, son of the Abbot, the clan held land in Perthshire. They were not Jacobites and the 15th chief was a major in the government army in 1745.

MacNaughten

There seems to be a clear link with the Pictish royal name of Nechtan and the clan held land around Killearn, north of Glasgow. They fought for James VII and II at Killiecrankie in 1689 with great ferocity.

MacNeil

Claiming descent from the great Irish king, Niall of the Nine Hostages (a reference to his holding power over nine kingdoms by taking hostages from their royal families), the MacNeils held Barra and parts of South Uist. In 1652 the chief and his priest returned Barra to the Catholic faith, but they suffered in the aftermath of the Jacobite rebellions. In 1937 Robert MacNeil came home from North America to reclaim and renovate the beautiful Kisimul Castle at Castlebay. His son is now chief of the clan.

MacNicol

As Nicolson the clan name better reveals its Norse origins. They held land on Lewis and later on Skye. Badly depleted by the Clearances, many Nicolsons and MacNicols settled in Australia.

MacPherson

Part of Clan Chattan, the MacPherson name comes from the Gaelic for son of the Parson; they originated in Badenoch. Ewan MacPherson of Cluny led part of the retreat from Derby in the 1745 rebellion and defeated a larger force of pursuers at Clifton Moor in Westmorland. Many reckon it to have been the last battle fought on English soil.

MacRae

Part of the Mackenzie alliance, the clan were keepers of the great castle of Eilean Donan on Loch Duich. They took no part in the rebellion of 1745, but 19th-century chiefs served in British armies with distinction.

Matheson

They held land in Lochalsh and Kintail, and were lieutenants of the Lords of the Isles. They did not support the Jacobite rebellions and turned their attention elsewhere. In 1827 Alexander Matheson and his uncle, James, founded the huge, far eastern trading company of Jardine Matheson.

Menzies

From Mesnières in France, the name was rendered as Manners in England and Menzies in Scotland. The clan held lands in Perthshire, at Atholl and Glenlyon. Perhaps their most glorious moment came at the battle at Killiecrankie when Major Duncan Menzies of Forlock led his clansmen in the charge that broke through the government ranks. But loyalties were divided and many of the Menzies men would have recognized their neighbours who fought against them. The present chief lives in Australia and Menzies Castle has been restored by the Clan Society, one of many creative acts carried out in the Highlands by the diaspora of clansmen of many names.

Morrison

A Hebridean clan of Irish descent, the Morrisons had a reputation as brehons or judges in the oral legal tradition of the Highlands. Involved in the war between the MacLeods and the Mackenzies for the island of Lewis, the clan lost their lands and military power.

MUNRO

Native to Easter Ross and the fertile coastal plain north of the Cromarty Firth, the clan had a proud martial tradition. Led by their chiefs, Munros fought in the armies of Gustavus Adolphus in the Thirty Years War in the 17th century. But they were not Jacobites.

MURRAY

The derivation of the name is simple. It comes from Moray and the Murrays of Tullibardine originated there before moving south to Perthshire. They became Dukes of Atholl and the fifth son of the 1st Duke was Lord George Murray, the talented general ignored by Prince Charles at Culloden. His elder brother, heir of the title, supported the government. Lord George had the distinction of being involved in the 1715 rebellion, the abortive campaign which ended at the battle of Glenshiel in 1719 (where he commanded the right wing at the age of 25) and in the 1745 rebellion. When he led a charge at Culloden, without his horse and his wig, Murray was 51. When Prince Charles made good escape to Europe in 1746, Lord George went to see him in Paris the following year. The Prince refused to see his old commander. Murray died in Holland in 1760.

OGILVY

Unusually the name may derive from an Old English root meaning high plains. The clan held land in Angus, but lost it after Culloden. But reconciliation did eventually come when the Hon. Angus Ogilvie, brother of the clan chief, married Princess Alexandra.

OLIPHANT

A Norman-French clan, they settled ultimately in Perthshire and were exiled after the last Jacobite rebellion in 1745. Carolina Oliphant wrote both of the most famous Jacobite songs, *Charlie is My Darlin'* and *Will Ye No Come Back Again*.

ROBERTSON

More correctly known as Clan Donnachaidh, or Clan Duncan, the Roberstons took their name from Robert of Atholl and they held land in Struan in Perthshire. Perhaps the most constant of all the clans in the Jacobite cause, they came out at each rebellion. Alexander Roberston, known as the Poet Chief, was captured twice by government troops after the 1715 rebellion and escaped twice. On his return from exile in 1725 he refused to swear an oath of allegiance to the Hanoverians. By 1745 Alexander was too old to fight, but it was said that he came to the battlefield at Prestonpans in his fur-lined nightshirt to watch, and was taken home in a captured English coach. The clan lands are long sold off; the line of chiefs lived in Jamaica before returning to live in England.

ROSS

Probably named after the great peninsula (*ros* in Gaelic) between the Dornoch and Cromarty Firths, the clan supported the Stuarts and were great magnates as the Earls of Ross. Unusually the line of chiefs has survived into modern times.

STEWART OF APPIN

The main branch of the family became kings of Scotland and Great Britain and Ireland, but the Appin Stewarts developed into a distinct Highland clan. Supporting their kinsmen in 1715 and 1745, they lost their lands and the chief was attainted for treason and exiled. There were Stewarts in Atholl, descended from Alexander Stewart, the Wolf of Badenoch and the name is now very common in Scotland.

URQUHART

The name is a Gaelic derivative probably meaning something like the fort on a knoll, which is what Castle Urquhart is, by the shore of Loch Ness. The chiefs were colourful figures. Sir Thomas Urquhart of Cromarty fought for Charles I and the cavalier army and also translated the works of the French poet, Rabelais. Captain John Urquhart of Craigston was known as 'The Pirate' since he was unwilling to divulge the source of sudden and great wealth. An American, Kenneth Urquhart, is now the 26th chief of the clan.

WALLACE

Perhaps the only Welsh clan name, it derives from Le Waleis, which had nothing to do with Wales or Welshmen but denoted a speaker of Old Welsh, the tongue of the ancient kingdom of Strathclyde and the other kingdoms of Dark Ages southern Scotland. The most famous scion was William Wallace, leader of the resistance to English occupation in the late 13th and early 14th centuries.

CLAN TARTANS

There are thousands of registered tartans, and it is beyond the scope of this volume to include every variation. If you would like to learn more, the Scottish Tartans Authority's International Tartans Index offers the most authoritative and comprehensive list; its searchable database of over 5,000 entries can be accessed online at http://www.tartansauthority.com/tartan-ferret/.

SOURCES OF ILLUSTRATIONS

FURTHER READING

Devine, Tom, *The Scottish Nation, 1700–2000*, London, 1999

Hunter, James, *A Dance Called America: the Scottish Highlands, the United States and Canada*, Edinburgh, 1994

——, *The Last of the Free: a Millennial History of the Highlands and Islands of Scotland*, Edinburgh, 1999

Lynch, Michael, *Scotland: A New History*, London, 1991

MacDonald, Donald, *Lewis, A History of the Island*, Edinburgh, 1978

MacLean, Fitzroy, *Highlanders*, London, 1995

MacLeod, John, *Highlanders: a History of the Gaels*, London, 1996

Prebble, John, *Culloden*, London, 1961 and New York, 1962

——, *Glencoe: the Story of the Massacre*, London and New York, 1966

Tacitus, Cornelius, *Agricola*, trans A. R. Birley, Oxford, 1999

Thomson, Derick S., *The Companion to Gaelic Scotland*, Glasgow, 1994

INDEX

Page numbers in *italics* refer to illustrations

Albert, Prince 119, 122; *118*
Anne, Queen 85

Bannockburn, Battle of 12, 32–33, 152, 153, 155, 161; *34*
Beaton 150
Blair 150
Brodie 150
Bruce 150
Buchan 150
Buchanan 150, 152
Burnett 150

Cameron 10, 41, 47, 58, 66, 69, 77, 79–80, 88, 95, 100, 108, 133, 151; *78, 94*
Campbell 7, 11, 31, 55, 64–74, 85, 86, 88, 91, 92, 108, 122, 147, 151, 156, 160, 161, 163, 165, 168; *30, 70*
Carmichael 11, 151
Cattanach 152
Charles I 64–65, 66, 173

Charles II 71, 150, 156
Chisholm 12, 114, 147, 152
Clan Chattan 12, 13–14, 29, 41, 75, 103, 147, 151–52, 153, 160, 164, 171
Clan Donald 7, 12, 31, 32, 35, 165
Clan Gregor 112, 113, 157; *158–59*
Clan Ranald 12, 32, 46, 47–48, 66, 71–72, 81, 104
Cleland 79
Colquhoun 152
Comyn 150, 152, 163
Culloden, Battle of 8–14, 35, 93, 100, 104, 108, 110, 112, 121, 136, 146, 161, 164, 168, 170, 172; *9, 10*
Cumberland, Duke of 9, 23
Cumming see Comyn

Davidson 152
Donald 153, 161
Donaldson see Donald
Drummond 11, 55, 153
Drummossie Moor 8–14, 101

Erskine 85–89, 153; *83*

Falkirk 8, 13, 40, 101
Farquharson 12, 152, 153
Fergusson 154
Field of the Shirts 48, 162
Forbes 154
Fraser 11, 12, 47–48, 68, 91, 103, 112, 137, 147, 150, 155

Galbraith 155
George I 85, 91
George II 92, 93, 96
George III 133
George IV 113, 116–17, 162, 164, 165; *115, 158–59*
Glencoe, Massacre of 64–74; *74*
Glen Shiel, Battle of 61, 172; *62–63*
Gordon 155
Graham 58, 64–74; *60, 66, 69*
Grant 12, 42, 47, 55, 91, 147, 155, 157; *39*
Gunn 147, 155

Hay 150, 156
Henderson 156

Innes 156

Jacobite rebellions 7, 11, 12,
40, 42, 56–58, 61, 75–105,
115, 119, 151, 153, 154, 155,
156, 157, 161, 162, 164, 165,
168, 170, 171, 172, 173; 62–
63, 86–87
James V 46
James VI and I 53, 55, 164; 54
James VII and II 56, 72, 80,
153, 170; 73
James VIII and III 38, 80, 81,
86, 88–93, 94; 89

Keith 150, 156
Killiecrankie, Battle of 57

Lamont 31, 156
Leckie 157
Lindsay 157
Livingstone 11, 157
Lovat 11–12, 47, 48

MacAlister 157
MacAllan 157
MacAlpine 157
MacArthur 157
MacAskill 160
MacAulay 12, 147, 160
MacBain 12, 152, 160
MacBane 75–76
MacBean 103, 152
MacBeth 160, 163
MacCaig 160
MacCallum 160–61
MacCoinneach 165
MacColl 11, 161
MacColla 24, 64–74, 160, 169
MacCombie 152
MacCrimmon 38, 40, 161,
170
MacDiarmid 161
MacDonald 7, 12, 14, 25, 32,
33, 35–36, 38, 42, 47, 49, 61,
64–74, 75, 76, 77, 81, 86, 95,
104, 108, 123, 127–28, 133,

136, 141, 143, 147, 153, 156,
157, 161; 102
MacDonald of Clan Ranald
162
MacDonald of Keppoch 12,
47, 75, 86, 95, 104
MacDonald of Sleat 81, 162
MacDonell of Glengarry 96,
162
MacDonnell 38, 67
MacDougall 32, 33, 163
MacDowall 163
MacDuff 163
MacEwan 163
MacFarlane 163–64
MacFie 164
MacGillivray 12, 152, 164
MacGregor 10, 55–56, 58–
61, 85, 89, 92, 112–13, 160,
164; 59
MacIain 12
MacIan 72, 74
MacInnes 164
MacIntyre 164
MacIver 108, 165
MacIvor 12, 147
MacKay 57–58, 77, 80, 130,
156, 165
MacKenneth 165
Mackenzie 22, 53, 67, 75, 114,
160, 162, 165, 169, 171
MacKinnon 35, 165–68; 35
Mackintosh 12, 14, 75, 76, 86,
87, 96, 98, 153, 168
MacLachlan 31, 168
MacLaine 35, 168
MacLaren 168
MacLay 11, 31
MacLean 12, 35, 71–72, 133,
138, 168–69; 37
MacLennan 169
MacLeod 7, 8–10, 12, 14, 35,
49, 51–53, 81, 95, 133, 136–
37, 138, 147, 160, 161, 169–
70, 171
MacMillan 170
MacNab 170
MacNaughten 170
MacNaughton 130
MacNeil 170

MacNeill 31, 35
MacNicol 171
MacPhail 152
MacPherson 109–10, 113,
152, 161, 171
MacRae 58, 133, 165, 171
MacRuari 32, 35
MacSween 12, 38, 147
MacThomas 152
Matheson 171
Menzies 10, 12, 42, 147, 171
Morrison 171
Munro 91, 172
Murray 10, 11, 13, 55, 80, 98,
99, 101, 172; 11

Ogilvy 172
Oliphant 172

Prestonpans, Battle of 8, 13,
100, 172–73
Prince Charles (also known
as Bonnie Prince Charlie)
8, 10, 12, 13, 14, 94, 95–105,
117, 133–36, 142, 151, 153,
156, 168, 172; 9, 97, 101, 143

Ritchie 152
Robert the Bruce 12, 27, 32,
33, 42, 64, 152, 161, 163; 26
Robertson 10, 172–73
Ross 173

Scott, Sir Walter 14, 61, 115–
16, 162
Shaw 151
Stevenson, Robert Louis 93
Stewart 93, 122, 133, 147
Stewart of Appin 11, 14, 66,
67, 173

Urquhart 47, 173; 169

Victoria, Queen 119–23, 127;
118

Wallace 173
William of Orange and Mary
II 56, 72, 80, 85, 151